CREATING A HOME

## PRACTICAL
# HOUSE REPAIRS

**Ward Lock Limited**
London

# CONTENTS

| | |
|---|---|
| **5** | Introduction |
| **7** | Fixing to wood and masonry |
| **11** | Hanging shelves |
| **15** | Wall-hung shelving |
| **17** | Renovating old doors |
| **21** | Problems with doors |
| **25** | Renovating cupboard doors |
| **29** | Replacing the woodwork |
| **33** | Cladding walls with timber |
| **37** | Choosing wood by the metre |
| **39** | Simple chair repairs |
| **43** | Renovating old furniture |
| **47** | Stripping and refinishing wood |
| **51** | Bambooing and vinegar graining |
| **55** | Wood finishes: traditional looks |
| **59** | Renovating iron and steel |
| **63** | Renovating brass, copper or bronze |
| **67** | Laying cork and vinyl floor tiles |
| **71** | Laying sheet flooring |
| **75** | Laying woodstrip flooring |
| **79** | Mosaic and wood sheet flooring |
| **83** | Renovating wood floors |
| **87** | Looking after the outside |
| **89** | Exterior decorating |
| **93** | Exterior door furniture |
| **95** | Index/Photographic credits |

© Ward Lock Limited, 1989
8 Clifford Street, London W1X 1RB, an Egmont Company

Based on *Creating a Home*,
First Edition © Eaglemoss Publications Limited, 1986.

All rights reserved. No part of this book may be reproduced, stored in a retrieval system or transmitted in any form or by any means, electronic, electrostatic, magnetic tape, mechanical, photocopying, recording or otherwise, without permission in writing from the publishers.

ISBN 0 7063 6731 6

Printed in Great Britain by Cooper Clegg Limited

# INTRODUCTION

Armed with a copy of this book, even the complete DIY beginner will soon be able to carry out a multitude of jobs around the house. It covers dozens of DIY projects, each explained in easy-to-follow, step-by-step form with illustrations and photographs showing the effects which can be achieved.

**Practical House Repairs** starts right where most new owners do: putting up shelves. A buyers' guide illustrates the varied range of shelving systems and brackets on the market. Next it tells you how to tackle simple jobs like renovating old doors, and more ambitious projects such as replacing skirting boards, door architraves and picture rails. Another buyers' guide illustrates the wide range of timber and mouldings on the market.

The floor makes up a large part of the surface area of any room, so making improvements here pays big dividends. More step-by-step drawings show how to lay vinyl tiles, cork tiles and sheet flooring like a professional. Or, if you prefer a timber floor, there are chapters on renovating floorboards and covering them with hardwood blocks.

**Practical House Repairs** also shows you how to repair and renovate furniture and fittings around the house. Detailed instructions explain how to repair old chairs; renovate the existing finish on wooden furniture or strip it off and apply a new one; plus how to renovate metals. In the final chapters the book turns to the outside: how to save money by tackling repairs to roofs, walls, woodwork and rainwater goods; and how to carry out your own exterior redecoration programme.

This is the ideal book for new home owners who want to know enough about DIY to carry out their own basic repair and renovation work.

# FIXING TO WOOD AND MASONRY

If you want shelves, and the like, to stay up, make sure you use the right fixing for the job.

Fixing one object to another – putting up a curtain track or a shelf, for example – are common DIY tasks.

This chapter covers fixing things with screws. Screws give a stronger fixing than nails, and a neater finish. Another advantage is that screwed fixings can be unscrewed and dismantled easily.

The simplest screw fixing is made into wood – all you have to do is make a small pilot hole to guide the screw as it cuts a thread in the wood fibres.

Screw fixings in masonry walls require a pre-drilled hole filled with a plug which gives the screw something to turn in and get a good grip. If the wall is hollow, the fixing is made through the wall with a special hollow wall fixing device.

## IDENTIFY THE WALL

Tap along the wall lightly with the handle of a screwdriver, or use your knuckles. If it is a hollow wall, there will be a change in sound between the plaster cladding and the solid timber uprights.

**Hollow walls** are either a timber framework of upright studs faced with plasterboard – a new partition wall, for example – or, in older homes, plaster over horizontal wooden slats (known as lath and plaster).

Use a bradawl, or make a test drilling, to determine the thickness of the cladding: plasterboard is 10-13mm thick; plaster on timber laths measures up to 18mm thick.

**Solid walls** are built of brick, block or concrete skimmed with plaster. If the dust from a drilled hole is red or yellow, the wall is brick; if it's grey, the wall is block. If it is very difficult to drill holes at all, it is probably concrete.

## TOOLS AND EQUIPMENT

**Screws** come in a range of sizes, materials and finishes. There are also several types of screw for specific purposes – see overleaf.

The size of screw is specified by its length in inches, and by diameter of the shank (the part between the head and the thread) which has a gauge number. The higher the gauge number, the thicker the screw. As a rough guide, ¾in No 8 gauge screws will cope with light loads, 1in No 10 with medium loads, and 1½in No 12 with heavy loads.

Most screws are made of steel. Brass screws are decorative but not as strong.

**A drill** is essential for making holes in wood or masonry. A hand drill can be slow but easier to control than a power drill. A 2-speed electric drill is worth buying if you expect to do lots of DIY; some drills have a hammer action that can be switched in to make drilling hard materials, such as concrete, easier.

The drilling tool is the 'bit'. There are different types of bit to suit the material to be drilled – see overleaf. When drilling into walls, always match bit size to plug size.

**A bradawl** can be used to make pilot holes in wood for small screws.

**Wallplugs** are essential when fixing to solid walls – they expand when a screw is driven in to provide grip. Moulded plastic plugs are most convenient to use – they have a small lip that sits flush with

*Kitchen display*
*Wooden battens and decorative wrought iron brackets are screwed to the wall to provide ample shelf and hanging space for a display of kitchen utensils.*

*Screw fixings into masonry walls are made with plastic plugs inserted into drilled holes.*

the wall surface, and most take a range of screw sizes.

**Plugging compound** is used for repairing badly drilled holes in solid walls. It is sold as powder to be mixed with water to a stiff paste.

**Hollow wall fixings** hold screws in the plaster cladding of hollow walls – they open behind the wall panelling to spread the load and prevent the fixing from pulling out. The fixing must be long enough to cope with the thickness of the cladding.

There are various designs but a collapsible plastic anchor is suitable for most jobs; special anchors for hollow doors are available.

**Screwdrivers** – use screwdrivers with a straight-tipped blade for slot-head screws; cross-head screwdrivers with a point to match Pozidriv or similar cross-head screws.

Always use a screwdriver of the right size for the screw – too wide or too narrow a blade will damage the head of the screw.

☐ You will also need a steel rule and a pencil for marking up drilling points accurately; a try-square is useful when drilling at right angles.

### CHECK YOUR NEEDS
☐ Screws
☐ Screwdriver to match type and size of screw
☐ Retractable steel rule and pencil
☐ Adhesive tape
☐ Try-square (optional)

**For masonry**
☐ Electric drill
☐ Masonry bit to match size of plug or fixing device
☐ Moulded plastic wallplug (for solid walls) or
☐ Hollow wall fixing device
☐ Plugging compound (optional)

**For wood**
☐ Bradawl (to make pilot holes for small screws)
☐ Hand or electric drill
☐ Twist drill bits (to make pilot holes for larger screws)

### SCREW TYPES
There are two basic types of screw: round-head and countersunk (with a flat head). Both are available with cross-head or single-slot drives. Cross-head screws require a special screwdriver but are easiest to drive in and remove.

**Countersunk** – use where head must be flush with the surface, such as on hinges.

**Raised countersunk** – neat appearance; use for fixing decorative hardware such as door handle plates.

**Domed head** – the cap fits into a countersunk screw head; use as decorative fixing for mirrors and bath panels.

**Round-head** – head protrudes from surface; use for fixing materials, such as thin metal, that cannot be countersunk.

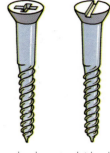
cross-head   slot-head

countersunk

raised countersunk

round-head

domed head

### SAFETY
Walls often conceal electric cables and plumbing pipes. NEVER drill fixing holes immediately around switches, lights or socket outlets, or anywhere near radiators and plumbing equipment if you can't see how the pipework reaches them.

### DRILL BITS

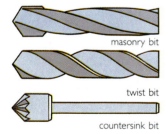
masonry bit
twist bit
countersink bit

**Masonry bits** have a hardened tip for drilling brick, block, and tiles; use an impact-type bit with a hammer-action drill for drilling concrete.

**Twist bits** are used for drilling wood, and will also cope with plasterboard. They come in a range of sizes.

**Countersink bits** are used to taper a hole so that the head of a countersunk screw will lie flush with the surface.

### USING A DRILL
Drilling is a skill essential to most fixing jobs. Here are some tips.

**Drilling wood**
Rest the wood you are drilling on scrap wood to prevent damage when the bit breaks through.

**Drilling a wall**
Use a nail to mark a starting point, or turn the drill bit by hand to make an indentation.

**Use a steady pressure**
When working with an electric drill, always use a firm, steady pressure – don't use excessive force to make it work faster or it will overheat. In general you need a high speed for drilling wood, a slow speed for masonry.

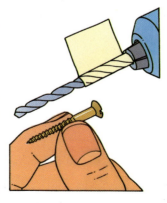

**Drill to the right depth** △
Measure the length of the screw against the bit to establish the depth of hole needed.

Some drills have a depth guide bolt for screwing on to the bit. If not, mark the length by winding a piece of adhesive tape round the bit. Don't let the tape ride up the bit when drilling.

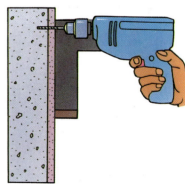

**Drill at right angles** △
Always keep the drill at right angles to the surface being drilled. Where possible, get a second person to hold a try-square against the wall with its blade pointing outwards alongside the drill as a guide.

## FIXING TO SOLID WALLS

Use an electric drill with a masonry bit to make a hole for the wallplug. In very hard surfaces, such as concrete, use a hammer-action drill with an impact-type masonry bit.

### 1 Drill a hole
Mark your drilling position on the wall with a nail or drill bit. Drill at slow speed, withdrawing the bit every so often to allow it to cool.

### 2 Insert the wallplug
Clear away loose dust. Then push the wallplug into the hole, tapping it in gently with a hammer so that its rim is flush with the surface of the wall. If the plug is too long, cut off the tapered bottom rather than the top – if it is still sticking out a little, trim off the excess plastic with a sharp knife.

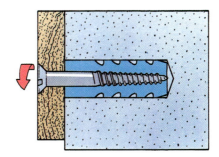

### 3 Drive in the screw △
Position the item you are fixing, insert the screw and drive it into the wallplug using a screwdriver.

## PLUGGING COMPOUND

Plugging compound is used to fill holes in soft walls that will not hold a wallplug. Apply the compound with a knife, ramming it in with a pencil. Then drive in screw.

The compound will start to set almost at once; remove the screw before it is fully set, and make the fixing by screwing into the hole.

## FIXING ABOVE WINDOWS

Fixings above windows, or to the underside of window reveals, can pose a problem if there is a load-bearing beam (a lintel) of hard concrete over the opening.

Instead of struggling to make holes coincide with fixing positions on curtain track, for example, it is often simpler to attach a wooden batten to the wall first. This allows greater flexibility when positioning the fixings on the wall, and may cut down the number of holes to be drilled and plugged in the concrete.

Screw the track directly to the wooden batten (see Fixing to wood, overleaf) and disguise the batten with paint or wallpaper to match the wall.

## FIXING TO HOLLOW WALLS

Use a hollow wall fixing device to attach light objects to the plaster cladding of the wall.

### 1 Drill a hole
Mark the drilling position. Drill a hole right through to the cavity, just large enough to take a fixing device of the appropriate size.

### 2 Slot in the fixing ▷
Slot the device through the hole – take care not to drop it through into the cavity. Position the item you are fixing and drive in the fixing screw.

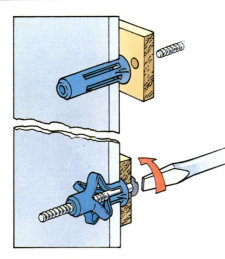

## HEAVY LOADS

For heavy fixings, screw into the supporting timber studs. If they are not in the right place, bridge two or more with a wooden batten and make your final fixings into that.

Locate the studs behind the plaster by tapping along the wall, and mark fixing positions with a pencil. Drill a pilot hole (as for wood) through the plaster skin, and drive the screw directly into the timber. Make sure the screw is long enough to penetrate the plasterboard (10 to 13mm thick) or lath and plaster (up to 18mm thick) and pass into the wood behind.

## FIXING TO CEILINGS

Always fix fittings to the timber joists supporting the ceiling.

### 1 Locate the joists
Decide where you want the fixing, then try to locate the nearest joist by tapping the ceiling – there will be a dull sound at each joist. Mark the position with a pencil.

If you can't find the joist, and you have access to the floor above, measure from the wall to the position of the fixing. Lift the floorboards at this point (or look in the loft) and poke a bradawl through the ceiling on both sides of the nearest joist.

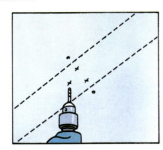

### 2 Fix to the joists △
Working within your test area, mark with a pencil the position of the drilling holes on the ceiling. Make sure that they are central on the joist.

Drill pilot holes for the fixing screws (as for wood) through the plaster skim of the ceiling into the joist. Attach the fitting with screws driven directly into the timber.

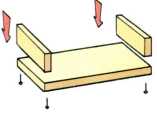

## FIXING BETWEEN JOISTS △

If the joists are not in the right place, it is possible to make a fixing between the joists if you have access to the floor above the ceiling.

Use a wooden batten (or larger panel of chipboard for heavy items) to bridge two joists and take the weight of the fitting.

Work out the position for the fitting, then remove the relevant floorboards in the room above. Cut the wooden batten to fit between the joists. Then screw or nail two small pieces of wood into both ends of the batten, and screw through these into the joists.

Mark and make a pilot hole through the ceiling, and attach the fitting by screwing into the batten.

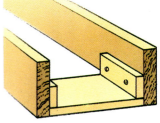

9

## FIXING TO WOOD

**1 Make a pilot hole**
To avoid splitting wood with a screw, make a pilot hole in the surface you are fixing to. It should be slightly shallower than the length of the screw threads and slightly smaller in diameter, so that the screw will 'bite' into the wood.

Use a bradawl for small screws. For screws gauge 6 or more, drill holes with a twist bit – see table below.

### DRILL BIT SIZES FOR PILOT HOLES

| Screw gauge | Drill bit size for: | |
|---|---|---|
| | Hardwood | Softwood |
| 4 | 1.5mm | bradawl |
| 6 | 2mm | 1.5mm |
| 8 | 2.5mm | 2mm |
| 10 | 2.5mm | 2mm |
| 12 | 3mm | 2.5mm |

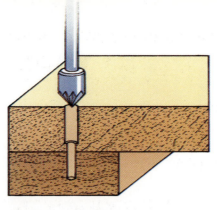

**2 Using a countersink bit** △
If you're using countersunk screws, you may have to taper the top of the hole in the object you are fixing with a drill and countersink bit.

This will ensure that the head of the screw can be driven in flush with the surface – particularly if the object you are fixing is metal or hardwood. If it is made of softwood, tightening the screw may be enough to pull the head flush into the wood.

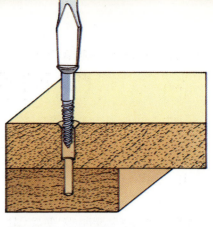

**3 Drive in the screw**
Thread the screw through the hole in the object you are fixing. Then secure the screw in the pilot hole using a screwdriver – to make it easier, lubricate the screw lightly with wax or grease before putting it in. Take care not to overtighten it.

With brass screws – which are weak – use a steel screw of the same size first to open out the pilot hole, then replace with the brass screw.

## USING A BRADAWL

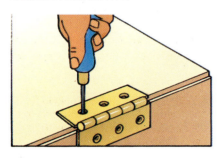

For small screws (up to gauge No 4), use a bradawl instead of a drill to make the pilot hole. Press the tip of the bradawl into the wood with a twisting action so that it cuts through the fibres and leaves a clean hole at the fixing point. Be careful not to make the hole too large.

### BRIGHT IDEA

**FIXING IN AWKWARD PLACES**
If a screw is difficult to hold while tightening, fit a short piece of rubber tubing over the tip of your screwdriver and push the head of the screw into the other end.

*Decorative detail*
China door fittings look decorative and are easily fixed into wood.

# HANGING SHELVES

Shelves provide essential storage and display space, and it requires very little skill to hang some on your walls.

Most homes need shelves of some sort – perhaps a single shelf for the telephone, or banks of shelves for a collection of books or records.

This chapter covers three basic methods of supporting wall-mounted shelves – adjustable bracket systems, fixed brackets and wooden battens. For how to make secure fixings to a wall, see previous chapter.

### FIXED OR ADJUSTABLE SHELVING?
The advantage of an adjustable system over fixed shelves is that once the uprights have been fixed to the wall, the shelves can be moved and added to when necessary. However, fixed shelves often look neater for display purposes.
**Adjustable shelving systems** consist of uprights that are fixed vertically to the wall, plus brackets that clip or slot into the uprights to support the shelves.

Most systems are made of aluminium with a coloured finish but wooden ones are also available. The length of upright dictates the height of shelving, and brackets are matched to the width of the shelves. Use brackets with a lip at one end for glass shelving.
**Fixed shelves** rest on supports screwed directly to the wall. One of the simplest supports is the L-shaped bracket, while wooden battens are ideal for shelves in alcoves.

Brackets come in a wide range of styles and materials – from traditional scrolled iron or wooden ones to modern designs of aluminium or bright-coloured enamelled steel. Most brackets come in sizes to take standard shelf widths with a supporting arm that is slightly shorter than the shelf depth. Some brackets are the width of the shelf with a lip to hold it.
**How much support?** The number of uprights or brackets you need, and the spacing between them, depends on the strength of the shelf material and the weight to be supported.

### SHELVING MATERIALS
Shelves can be bought in standard sizes, or you can have them cut to length – most timber merchants and large DIY stores offer this service.

The type of material you choose depends on the weight the shelf will carry. All except plastic-faced shelves and glass should be treated with a protective finish so that they're easy to clean. Cut edges of manufactured boards need covering to give a neat finish.
**Solid wood** is strong and ideal for heavy loads, although likely to be expensive.
**Chipboard** is the least expensive, but it is relatively weak and needs more support than other shelving.

Wood-veneered and plastic-faced chipboard is available ready-finished in a range of shelf-sized widths (from 150mm upwards) and lengths. Ordinary chipboard can be painted; cut edges need to be covered.
**Plywood and blockboard** are sold mainly in large sheets, but you can have

*Versatile storage*
*Adjustable shelving easily adapts to meet changing storage needs. Here, uprights are fitted with white strips that conceal unused bracket slots.*

shelves cut to size. Both are available plain or with wood veneer or plastic facing; cut edges need to be covered. **Glass** is popular in bathrooms and also makes elegant display shelving. Order float glass at least 6mm thick and have the edges ground so that they can't cut; you'll need special brackets with a lip at one end to hold the glass in place.

## THE FIXINGS

Screws are required for fixing the shelf supports, plus wallplugs (for solid walls) or cavity fixings (for lightweight shelves on plasterboard walls). Depending on the size of the shelf and the load it will take, you will need 50mm, 62mm or 75mm-long fixing screws: No 6 screws are suitable for light weights; No 10 for heavy weights. Fixings are usually supplied with shelving kits.

If you need screws for fixing shelves to brackets, make sure their length is less than the board thickness so they won't burst through the top of the shelf.

### MAXIMUM DISTANCES BETWEEN SUPPORTS

Position end supports so that the shelf will extend on each side by about one-fifth of the total shelf length. For long shelves, the distance between supports should not exceed the distances given in the table below:

| SHELF MATERIAL | THICKNESS | MAXIMUM DISTANCE |
|---|---|---|
| Solid wood | 12mm | 450mm |
|  | 19mm | 600mm |
|  | 25mm | 1000mm |
| Chipboard | 12mm | 400mm |
|  | 18mm | 450mm |
| Plywood | 12mm | 450mm |
|  | 18mm | 600mm |
| Blockboard | 12mm | 450mm |
|  | 25mm | 750mm |
| Glass | 6mm | 450mm |

**Note:** These distances between supports are suitable for medium to heavy loads (eg. books or records). For lighter loads such as ornaments, etc, you can increase distances by up to a third.

## FIXING ADJUSTABLE SHELVING

Uprights come in a range of sizes, but they sometimes need shortening: if so, cut to size with a small hacksaw.

**1 Measure and mark the wall ▷**
To get the height of the shelves, hold one of the end uprights against the wall. Mark its top edge with a pencil, and use a spirit level and straight edge to lightly draw a horizontal line on the wall at this point.

Then measure off and mark the positions of adjacent uprights along the pencil line – for maximum distances between supports, see Table above.

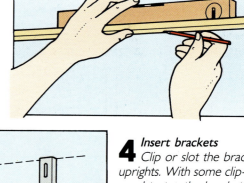

**2 Drill the top fixing hole ▷**
Align the top edge of each upright with the horizontal guideline on the wall, and use a pencil to mark the position of the top screw fixing hole.

Drill the holes, and plug with a wallplug or cavity fixing if necessary. Then fix each upright to the wall – but without tightening the fixing screw so that the upright is free to swing to a vertical.

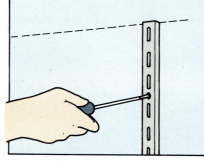

**3 Drill remaining fixing holes ▷**
With the upright hanging loosely against the wall, hold a spirit level against it to check that it is vertical and adjust if necessary. Mark the positions of all the remaining fixing holes through the upright on to the wall.

Holding the upright to one side, drill holes at each pencil mark. Then fit the plugs and screw the upright tightly into place (not forgetting to tighten the topmost screw). If the wall is uneven, fill any gaps behind the uprights with small pieces of cardboard before tightening screws.

Repeat the above for each upright.

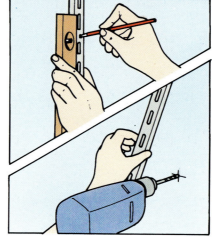

**4 Insert brackets**
Clip or slot the brackets into the uprights. With some clip-in systems you need to tap the bracket firmly into its slot with a mallet or a hammer – protect the bracket with a scrap of softwood.

If you use uprights with a continuous channel, hold the bracket at an angle so that its upper lug is engaged in the channel and the lower one is held clear. Then slide the bracket down to the required height and lower it to the horizontal position to lock it in place.

**5 Position the shelves**
Lay top shelf in position. Then hang a plumb line over one side edge and line up subsequent shelves with the string.

**6 Fix the shelves**
If there are screw holes, you can fix shelves securely. Mark fixing hole positions through brackets on to the underside of shelves. Remove shelves and brackets, screw together and replace into uprights in one piece.

## BRIGHT IDEA

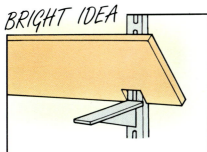

**FIT SHELVES FLUSH**
Cut small notches in the rear edge of each shelf with a tenon saw, and chisel out the waste so that it fits round the uprights. Then insert brackets and fix the shelves.

## CHECK YOUR NEEDS
- Adjustable shelving system OR shelf brackets OR wooden battens (25mm thick, 30-50mm deep)
- Shelves
- Fixing screws
- Wallplugs (solid walls) OR cavity fixings (hollow walls)
- Junior hacksaw (for cutting uprights to length)
- Pencil
- Spirit level/straight edge
- Steel tape measure
- Plumb line (or any small weight and string)
- Electric drill and bit
- Bradawl or small twist drill for making pilot holes in shelves
- Screwdriver
- Tenon saw and chisel for fitting shelves round uprights
- Block plane for trimming shelves

**For shelves made of manufactured board:**
- Iron-on edging strip OR timber lipping (plus glue and panel pins)
- Fine-grade glasspaper

## PUTTING UP FIXED SHELVING

The easiest method is to screw the brackets to the shelf and then to the wall, but it helps to have a second person holding the shelf horizontal while you mark the fixing hole positions.

**1 Mark the wall**
Decide the height of the shelving by holding the shelf against the wall. Make a pencil mark at its top edge, and use a spirit level to draw a horizontal line on the wall at this point.

**2 Fix the brackets** ▷
Determine spacing between brackets (see Table). Lay shelf upside down and draw a line at right angles to shelf edge for each bracket.
Position one bracket, with the shorter arm centred over the marked line and the longer arm flush with the rear edge of the shelf. Mark screw positions on to the shelf through the holes in the bracket arm, drill pilot holes and drive in fixing screws. Repeat for other brackets.

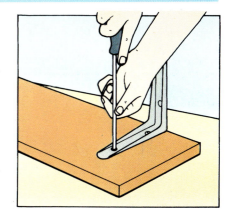

**3 Drill the fixing holes** ▷
Hold the shelf, complete with brackets, with its rear edge aligned with the pencil line on the wall and place a spirit level on top of the shelf to check that it's truly horizontal. Mark drilling positions with a pencil through the fixing holes in the brackets; lift shelf aside, drill fixing holes, and plug if necessary.

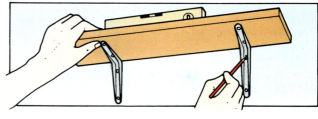

**4 Fix the shelf to the wall**
Holding the shelf firmly in position, drive in one fixing screw per bracket and tighten it halfway. Drive in the remaining fixing screws and tighten the whole lot up.

**Several shelves** If you're putting up a bank of shelves, fix the top shelf in position first. Then hang a plumb line over one short end and line up the shelves below with the string.

## FINISHING MANUFACTURED BOARDS

If your shelves are of manufactured board, neaten raw edges with plastic iron-on strip to match the existing veneer, or use a strip of plain or moulded timber lipping for a more attractive, durable finish.

### Timber lipping
This is available in various shapes and widths: cover the cut edges of boards with a strip of exactly the right width, or use a wider strip to conceal shelf fixings or display lighting fitted beneath shelf.
Glue the lipping to the raw edge. Then reinforce with small panel pins, punching the heads below the surface with a hammer and filling with wood stopping of a suitable colour. Sand smooth before applying finish.

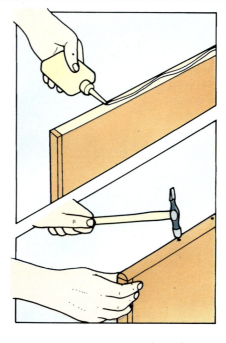

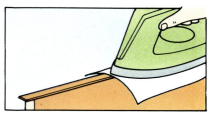

### Iron-on edging strip
Cut a piece of edging strip a little longer than the shelf. Position it over the raw edge, protect the surface of the strip with a piece of paper and press it firmly into place with a warm iron — for a couple of seconds, no longer.
Allow it to cool. Then trim off the ends of the strip with a craft knife, and smooth the edges with medium then fine-grade glasspaper wrapped round a sanding block. Angle the block slightly as you work to bevel edges of the strip.

## FITTING SHELVES IN ALCOVES

You can use brackets or adjustable shelving in alcoves, but it's cheaper and just as easy to support shelves with wood battens fixed to the walls of the alcove itself. If the side walls aren't perfectly straight you will have to trim and shape each shelf to fit.

### 1 Mark the wall ▷
Start by deciding the approximate position of each shelf, spacing them according to the height of the things you intend putting on them. Then draw pencil lines on the three walls of the alcove at each shelf position, using a spirit level to make sure the lines are horizontal.

If shelves are to be recessed into the alcove, hang a plumb line down the wall at the point where the front edge of the shelves will come and mark the position of each with a pencil. Check the width and depth measurements for each shelf; have shelves cut to fit.

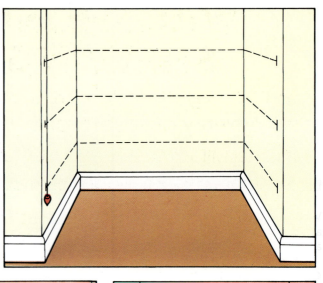

### 2 Cut the battens ▷
Cut two battens so that they're just shorter than the width of the shelf they're supporting. So that the battens look less obtrusive when the shelf is fitted, bevel their front ends with a saw cut at about 45 degrees and sand smooth.

Pre-drill fixing holes in each batten, and countersink them if necessary for the screw heads. Two screw holes will be enough unless the shelf is very deep: drill them 50mm in from the ends; then, if necessary, at 300mm intervals.

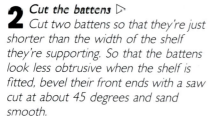

### 3 Fix the side battens △
Hold a batten against a side wall of the alcove with its top edge aligned with the pencil guideline. Mark the positions of the screw holes on to the wall. Drill the wall, plug the holes, and screw batten into position.

Repeat for the other batten.

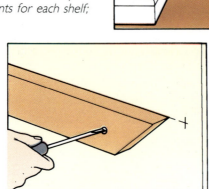

### A third batten △
If the alcove is relatively wide and/or the shelf will be carrying a heavy load, add a third support batten along the back wall of the alcove.

Cut it to fit flush with the rear edges of the side battens.

### 4 Position the shelf △
Place shelf in position and check that it's resting properly on the battens. If the side walls of the alcove are not square, trim the side ends of the shelf with a small block plane to get a good fit – work from both edges in towards the centre to avoid splitting the wood.

Now fix the battens for the other shelves, following Steps 2 and 3.

### Built-in shelves
An alcove provides an ideal site for neat, built-in shelving. Here supporting battens are fixed to all three walls to take a heavy load of books and records.

# WALL-HUNG SHELVING

Well designed wall-hung shelving can create plenty of additional storage space for keeping your home neat and tidy.

Wall-hung shelving is best positioned in a natural alcove, but it can be put almost anywhere within reason.

When buying shelving you can choose shelves made from solid wood, various man-made boards, glass or metal. You then have to decide how these shelves are to be supported: there are fixed brackets, adjustable brackets fitted to uprights, folding brackets or end-supports (for alcove shelving).

## SHELVING MATERIALS

**Wood** The most attractive solid wood shelves are made from hardwood such as teak or mahogany. But these are expensive and most shelves are made from softwoods such as pine or European redwood. There are several different grades of wood; for timber shelving, you need joinery grade. Wood is available for shelving in a range of widths going up in 25mm (1in) grades to 300mm (12in) and in 12mm (½in), 19mm (¾in) and 25mm (1in) thicknesses. The size of timber given is *before* the wood is planed for a smooth finish. The finished size of timber is therefore around 3mm (⅛in) less than what is known as the nominal size.

**Man-made boards** Natural wood is expensive and many shelves are made from chipboard, which consists of wood chippings glued together. Plain chipboard is not very attractive even when painted, so for shelves you can use either melamine-faced or wood-veneered chipboard.

Both these are stronger than plain chipboard, but not as strong as solid wood. (Melamine is a plastic, and wood veneer is a very thin sheet of natural wood – typically teak or mahogany – glued to the surface of the chipboard). With both types, you can buy edging strips to cover ends where the board is cut and underlying chipboard exposed.

Melamine-faced and wood-veneered chipboard are sold in lengths from 1.8m (6ft) upwards and in 150mm (6in), 225mm (9in) and 300mm (12in) widths. The thickness is a standard 15mm (⁹⁄₁₆in).

Other man-made boards can also be used for shelving. These include blockboard (strips of wood glued together and covered with thin sheets of veneer) and plywood (thin sheets of veneer glued together). The grain of alternate layers goes in opposite directions, so both of these are stronger than natural wood.

Blockboard and plywood are sold in large sheets 2440mm × 1220mm (8ft × 4ft) and thicknesses usually range from 3mm (⅛in) to 25mm (1in). Medium-density fibreboard (MDF) can also be used. It has a smooth finish and sells in large sheets or 210mm (8¼in) widths. Thicknesses range from 6mm (¼in) to 25mm (1in).

**Glass** is an attractive shelving material – particularly for shelves used for decorative display rather than ordinary storage. The glass itself needs to be fairly thick, at least 6mm (¼in), and to be 'edge-treated' to give it smooth and slightly rounded edges and corners.

**Metal** shelves are usually found on floor-standing shelving units, although some manufacturers of adjustable wall shelving supply metal shelves as an option.

## SUPPORTING SHELVES

Whatever shelving material you choose, your shelves must be well supported so that they do not sag and come away from the wall. The maximum unsupported length of a shelf depends both on the material used (and its thickness) and the load which the shelf is expected to carry. As a general guide, see the table on page 12 for the maximum distances between supports.

## SHELVING METHODS

All shelving systems are based on three basic methods.

**Bridging method** The simplest way to fit shelves between two walls (in an alcove or cupboard). Shelves are supported at either end by battens or studs.

**Frame method** A framework supports the shelves at either end. Can be free-standing or fixed to a wall.

**Bracket method** The shelves are supported by brackets (often adjustable) which fit into uprights fixed to the wall.

---

### FIXED BRACKETS
**Style** Each shelf is fitted with its own brackets which are screwed either directly to the wall or to wooden battens in the wall.
**In use** For wooden shelves, you could make your own timber angle brackets. Otherwise the traditional steel bracket is painted grey and has a central rib to strengthen it, but there are more attractive brackets including ornate 'scroll' ones.
**Watchpoint** The main disadvantage of this type of bracket is that it takes a long time to put up – especially if you are putting up several shelves – as each shelf has to be individually levelled and each bracket screwed to the wall.

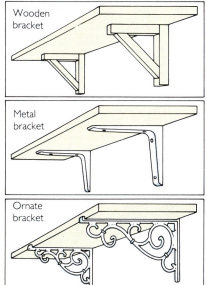

Wooden bracket

Metal bracket

Ornate bracket

### SLING BRACKET
**Style** An alternative to the L-shaped bracket underneath the shelf is a plastic sling above it. This has a single screw mounting supporting a plastic loop in which the shelf is fitted.
**In use** As there is only one screw needed per sling (and approximately two slings per shelf), these shelves are ideal for any situation where drilling into walls could be tricky. They are also good in old houses which have uneven, sloping walls as the sling is flexible and adapts to them. They make strong shelves, designed to take up to 51kg. The sling is suitable for wood, steel or glass shelves.

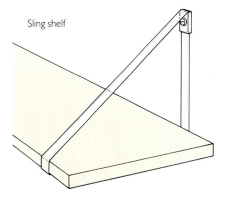

Sling shelf

## CANTILEVER BRACKETS

**Style** These shelf brackets are less obtrusive than ordinary brackets and can be used when fitting ordinary brackets is impractical – for a shelf over a radiator, for instance.
**The use** They rely for their support on a long hardened steel rod which goes into the wall. This means they can be used only on solid walls (or the studs of partition walls) and that a fairly large hole has to be drilled, which must be both straight (i.e. at right angles to the wall) and horizontal. The bracket is then pushed into the hole and held in place with a single screw.

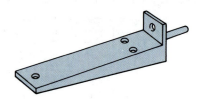

## SLOTTED-SUPPORT STRIP

**Style** A continuous triangular strip which is screwed to the wall.
**In use** The shelf is pushed into the slot, making a very unobtrusive support. Two versions are made in various lengths and colours: one for 15mm (9/16in) chipboard and one for 6mm (1/4in) glass.

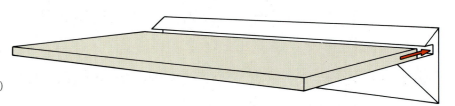

## ADJUSTABLE BRACKETS

**Style** Uprights are screwed to the wall and the shelf support brackets slotted into them. This means you can change the spacing of the shelves at will and there is the added advantage that once one shelf has been correctly levelled (with a spirit level), all the others will be level too.
**In use** Materials include natural timber, coloured aluminium and painted steel. Each manufacturer has his own design of bracket and upright, but they fall basically into two groups. In the first, the brackets fit into a single or double row of slots or holes in the upright, typically spaced 25mm to 50mm (1-2in) apart. In the second type, the bracket slides up a channel and can be positioned anywhere before being locked in place.

The uprights for adjustable shelving are sold in various lengths, and different sizes of bracket are available for different widths of shelf. Most manufacturers also provide heavyweight and heavy-duty brackets and sloping display brackets.
**Watchpoint** For safety, the shelves should be screwed to the bracket – most systems have a facility for doing this.

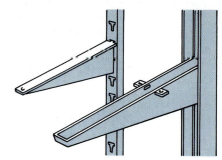

## ADJUSTABLE SHELVING EXTRAS

There are a number of accessories which you can buy to fit on to adjustable shelving systems to complement the shelves.
**Book ends** attach to the shelves to support your books and stop them falling off the end of the shelf (see left). Types on the market either have to be screwed to the shelf, fitted into holes drilled into the shelf, slid over the shelf or fitted into spare slots in the uprights.

**Storage** You can build up a whole wall of storage (as well as shelves) by attaching wire baskets, racks, (record racks), cabinets, and even drawers to adjustable systems.
**Other extras** There are also poles from which you can hang clothes hangers (see left), light fittings such as spotlights, where the flex runs inside the upright supports (see left), and even pegboards (ideal for hanging tools).

## CORD SUPPORTS

**Style** Medium-density fibreboard shelves supported by cords. Shelves can be hung at any position desired. Cord and shelves come in a variety of colours.
**In use** The side cords are fixed to two screws at the top, which take the load, and two at the bottom, which stop the shelves wobbling about. At each chosen shelf position, the cord is passed through the shelf to form a loop into which a chromium plated tube is inserted. Additional tubes can be used between shelves as book-ends.
**Watchpoint** The whole system is supported by just two screws. These must be firmly secured into a solid wall or a stud of a partition wall.

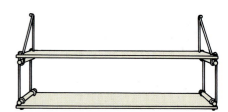

## FOLDING SHELF BRACKETS

**Style** A bracket which allows a shelf to be folded down out of the way.
**In use** Brackets for folding shelves incorporate a hinge and, usually, a jointed stay for holding the shelf upright. This type of bracket is available in a number of sizes – large enough to support a table or worktop which, when not in use, can be folded flat against the wall. It is an ideal bracket to use when space is limited.
**Watchpoint** With some types of folding bracket, you may have to secure the bracket to a horizontal piece of timber rather then screwing it directly to the wall.

## SHELF END SUPPORTS

**Style** These are supports which are fitted to the sides of a narrow alcove on which the shelf rests.
**In use** There are various types ranging from slotted metal strips with small studs which fit into them (also suitable for bookcases) to home-made wooden battens (which could also be used along the back of a shelf to provide support), metal or plastic end support studs screwed into the side walls (particularly suitable for bookcases) and special studs into which glass shelves are slotted (also available in clear perspex so they are camouflaged).

Angled metal strip can also be used to support shelves. If fitted into a groove in the end of the shelf, it will be concealed. Also available are wire supports which fit into a groove in the shelf and are completely concealed.

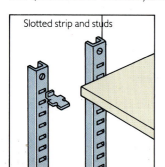
Slotted strip and studs

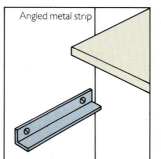
Angled metal strip

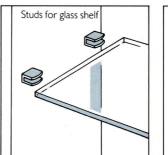
Studs for glass shelf

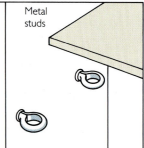
Metal studs

# RENOVATING OLD DOORS

Restoring old doors to their original condition keeps the style of a house and saves you money.

The doors in older homes reflect the style of the building as much as other fixtures and fittings, so it makes sense to try to retain them wherever possible.

However, over the years they may have suffered their fair share of wear and tear, and worse still, previous owners may have subjected them to terrible indignities such as adding extra door furniture or, worst of all, cladding them in hardboard or plywood to create the flush look so popular in newer homes. But all is not lost, and some simple repair and restoration work can often bring a thoroughly tatty-looking door back to something like its original condition.

**Panelled doors** The best thing about old doors is that they're made from solid wood – usually pine, but sometimes hardwood such as oak or mahogany in grander houses. A typical panelled door has two main vertical members called stiles, linked together by horizontal rails – one at top and bottom, and one or two across the centre, depending on whether the door has four or six panels. These in turn are linked by central vertical members called muntins, which divide the door up into panels. In houses built between the wars, the structure is basically the same, but the arrrangement of panels may vary (see below).

These spaces between the rails, stiles and muntins may be filled in with fielded (raised and mitred) panels on the grandest doors, or thinly-cut solid wood or glass on humbler types. Plywood may also be found, as a recent replacement for old panels that have split. The panel is either held in grooves in the surrounding stiles, rails and muntins or retained in rebates by planted (pinned-on) beading.

All the joints between these various members are usually of the mortice-and-tenon type (shown below), so the whole construction is solid and rigid. One stile is hinged to the door frame, and is called the hinge stile; the other is referred to as the opening stile, and is fitted with a latch or lock and door handles on each face of the door.

**Ledged and braced doors** You may also come across ledged and braced doors, which were commonly used in Victorian times for back doors and outhouses, and also as internal doors in artisan homes. These consist of vertical tongued-and-grooved boards fixed to top, centre (also known as the lock rail) and bottom rails, with the boards facing outwards; these three rails were themselves linked by two diagonal braces to prevent the door from sagging. Hinges usually had long straps which were screwed to the inner face of the top and bottom rails; a surface-mounted

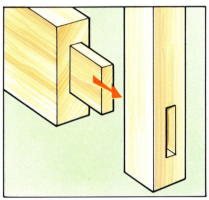
*Mortice-and-tenon joint*

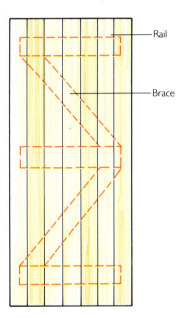
*Ledged and braced door*

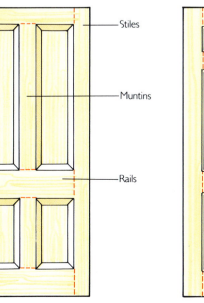
*Four-panelled door (Victorian)*

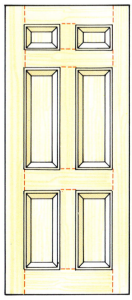
*Six-panelled door (Georgian)*

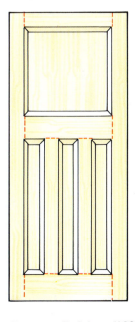
*Four-panelled door (1930s)*

rim lock was fitted to the lock rail.

**Flush doors** became popular only after about 1945, and any that are found in older houses are either replacements or the product of the flush-facing treatment mentioned earlier. The former can be given a panelled look by the addition of surface moulding, while the latter can be restored by the simple expedient of removing the facing board (see below).

All modern flush doors have a frame – two stiles, two rails – which is covered on each face with hardboard or plywood. The centre of the door is usually filled with lightweight honeycomb packing, and there is a lock block fitted inside the frame on one or both edges of the door, about half-way up. Because of the hollow core, fixing things like coat hooks involves having to use special cavity fixing devices (see page 9) as plain screws simply pull out.

**Modern panelled doors.** Again fitted as replacements for the original, but with some attempt at retaining the house's style. These may be mass-produced types with a proper frame, but are more likely to be flush doors with moulded fibreboard panels.

## TOOLS AND EQUIPMENT

None of the tasks described here need any special tools. However, if you are thinking of giving a flush door a panelled look, it is a good idea to look at the various kits available in DIY stores, as well as the more traditional beading available by the metre.

### EXPOSING A PANELLED DOOR

**1** *Prise up a corner ▷*
To remove a hardboard or plywood facing, try to insert a knife or scraper blade between the facing and the door itself near a corner. If the blade slides in fairly easily once you've cut through the paint film, work it sideways until you meet the first panel pin, and try to lever the facing away. Usually the facing pulls away, leaving the pin in place.

If the knife won't go in or you can't prise up the corner of the facing, this suggests that the panel may have been glued on. Try playing heat from a hot air gun over the surface of the panel while trying to prise up a corner; this may soften old scotch glue enough for you to release the panel. If modern woodworking adhesive has been used, removing the panel is usually virtually impossible unless the door is immersed in water to soften the adhesive; it may be worth consulting a door stripping firm for advice.

If you can lift a corner, carry on in the same way along each edge until all are freed from the pins. Then pull off the panel – in sections if necessary; pins may have been driven into the door's centre rail and muntin too.

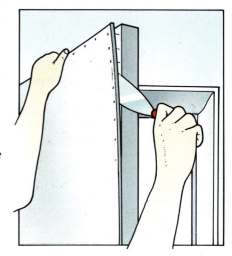

**2** *Pull out the pins ▷*
Use a pair of pincers to pull out all the old panel pins. Rest the pincer jaws on some card to avoid denting and marking the surface of the door. If any of the pins break, use a nail punch and hammer to drive the shaft of the pin right into the door by about 2mm.

At this stage, you should decide on how you are going to refinish the newly-exposed door surface. If you want a stripped wood door, strip the finish, or have the door dipped by a professional company for a few pounds. For a painted finish, sand down and clean the old paintwork to provide a key for the new finish.

**3** *Make good the door surface*
With all the pins removed (and the old finish stripped if required), make good all the pin holes and any other defects, such as cracked panels, loose beading, and scars from door handles and bolts which have been removed.

Use interior filler if you intend to repaint the door or wood stopper in a shade to match the wood colour if you plan to varnish it. You may need to experiment with wood stopper so that you tint it to a shade to match the varnished door rather than the stripped wood.

### CHECK YOUR NEEDS

**For exposing a panelled door:**
☐ Wide scraper or old, wide knife
☐ Pincers
☐ Nail punch and hammer
☐ Paint stripper, blowlamp or hot air gun (according to the finish required)
☐ Wood stopper to match door colour (for a natural finish) or interior filler (painted finish)
☐ Filling knife
☐ Glasspaper
☐ Paint or varnish
☐ Paintbrush

**For adding panels to flush doors:**
☐ Straightedge
☐ Tape measure
☐ Pencil
☐ Set square

**If you're adding beading:**
☐ Beading
☐ Mitre box
☐ Tenon saw
☐ Panel pins
☐ Pin hammer
☐ Nail punch and hammer OR
☐ Imitation door panels
☐ Panel adhesive

**For making warped doors fit:**
☐ Craft knife
☐ Nail punch and hammer
☐ Old chisel
☐ Pencil
☐ 38mm oval wire nails
☐ Filler

**For closing up split panels:**
☐ Dowel
☐ Electric drill
☐ Woodworking glue
☐ Saw
☐ Mallet
☐ Plane and glasspaper

## APPLYING BEADING TO A FLUSH DOOR

### 1 Mark up the door face
Plan your panel sizes on paper, then use brown paper templates to check the effect on your door. If you already have some panelled doors, use one of these as a model. Then use your straightedge, set square and pencil to mark the outline of each panel on the door face. This gives guidelines for when you come to fit the beading.

### 2 Mitre the beading
Start by mitring one end of your first length of beading as shown below. Then measure the width and height of each panel, and make a note of how many components you will need of each size. Mark the required length on the lengths of beading, measuring from the outer edge of the first mitre, and cut the second mitre in the reverse direction. Make a fresh mitre on the end of the stock length, and continue cutting further sections to the required lengths. Sand the cut ends lightly to remove any splinters, but take care not to round off the mitre.

### 3 Pin on the beading ▷
On your bench, drive a panel pin in near each end of the first length of beading. Then offer it up to the door surface, aligning it with the pencil lines made earlier, and tap in the pins. Add intermediate pins as required.

Now offer up the remaining three lengths in turn to complete the first 'panel', aligning the mitres carefully and checking that the corners are square.

Complete the other panels in the same way, checking that verticals and horizontals are aligned across the door face. Then punch in and fill all the pin heads and fill any cracks in the mitred joints, ready for painting or varnishing.

### 4 Paint or paper the panels
You can simply paint or stain and varnish the beading to match the rest of the door surface, but very attractive effects can be achieved by painting the beading (and/or the panels themselves) in a contrasting colour. Alternatively, you could echo the room's colour scheme by sticking pieces of matching wallpaper within the panels using ordinary wallpaper paste.

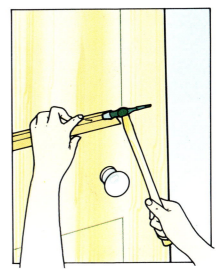

### 5 Stick on imitation panels
As an alternative, you can buy imitation fielded panels to stick to the face of flush doors. Start by marking their positions (see step 1), then apply the adhesive and press the panels into place. If they show any signs of slipping, hold them temporarily with masking tape. When the adhesive has set, fill any gaps between door and panels.

## USING A MITRE BOX ▷
Position the beading (or other item to be cut) in the mitre box, with the flat side on the floor of the box, and hold the most heavily moulded edge against one side of the box. Slip a flat piece of scrap wood under the beading, so that you can cut cleanly through the beading without damaging the floor of the box. Check which of the slots you are using to give you the correct angle on the mitre. Saw with the spine of the saw parallel to the top of the box and the blade absolutely vertical, taking care not to saw into the box itself.

When measuring subsequent lengths, measure and mark the longer, outer edge of the beading to be mitred. Position the marked length so that the mark matches the appropriate slot.

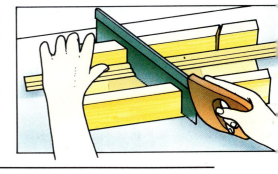

## MAKING WARPED DOORS FIT

### 1 Prise off the old door stops ◁
It's very difficult to correct a warped door, and an easier cure for the problem is to prise off and reposition the door stops against which the door closes in its frame (this obviously cannot be done where the stop is formed as a rebate in the frame).

Start by running a knife down the angle where the stop meets the frame, to cut through the paint film. Then try to locate the positions of the fixing nails, and drive them through into the door frame with a hammer and nail punch. Next, insert the chisel between stop and frame at the bottom, and prise it carefully away, working up towards the head of the frame. Repeat this movement to remove the stop across the door head, if necessary.

### 2 Mark the door position ▷
Rub down the damaged paintwork where the door stop has been removed, using a scraper to remove any lumps and bumps if necessary. Now close the door and make a pencil line on the frame carefully following the angle of the warped door edge.

### 3 Replace the door stop
Offer up the old door stop (or a new length of timber the same shape as the old one if the old stop was split or damaged during removal) and nail it into place against the marked line. Use tacks to fix it just at the top and bottom to start with, and close the door to check the fit. When you are satisfied with the angle of the door stop, drive in the remaining nails, punch in the nail heads slightly and make good.

## BRIGHT IDEA

**MAKING LIGHT WORK**
For a door into a kitchen or in a corridor, you can replace the wooden panels with glass. Remove the beading from round the panels, then, using a padsaw or jigsaw, cut out the panels close to the stiles, rails and muntins.

Buy sheets of toughened glass, exactly the same size as the opening. Fix them in place with solid hardwood beading, either quadrant or square. Screw the beading in place round one side of the opening, then fit the glass into the opening, holding it in place with putty. Screw more beading in place round the other side of the glass to hold it firmly.

## CLOSING UP SPLIT PANELS

**1 Drill into the door edge** ▽
Central heating and old age often lead to splits appearing in solid wood panels, and it's usually impossible to replace them without dismantling the door. It's easier to close them up by driving dowels sideways into the stile next to the panel so that as you knock the dowel in it pushes the sections of the panel together.

Select a twist drill to match the dowel diameter, and drill two holes into the door edge, deep enough to reach to the edge of the split panel (usually about 5mm less than the width of the door stile). It's a good idea to use a depth stop as a guide, and to finish off by drilling slowly so you don't damage the panel itself.

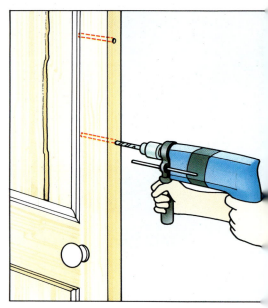

**2 Drive in the dowels**
First of all, use a knife to open up the split in the panel so you can spread some woodworking adhesive along the line of the split. Then cut the dowels a little longer than the width of the stile, apply glue to the end and tap each one into the hole with a mallet. When the dowel reaches the edge of the panel, it should close up the split. Using a damp cloth, wipe off any excess adhesive that oozes out.

**3 Trim off the excess**
Leave the glue to set. Then saw off the excess dowel as close to the door edge as you can, and plane and sand it flush for an almost invisible repair.

◁ **Polish up your doors**
Beautifully restored, and in this case stripped, panelled doors add to the character of a house. In a hallway, there are usually several doors, so make them a feature rather than an eyesore.

# PROBLEMS WITH DOORS

An ill-fitting creaky door, or one that opens the wrong way, are problems that can easily be solved.

Doors receive a lot of hard wear and over the years usually start to stick, squeak and rattle. These are all problems that can easily be put right.

Sometimes a door is inconveniently hung – on the wrong side of the frame, for example, so that it blocks the light when open or makes access to the room difficult. A simple remedy is to rehang the door so that it opens the opposite way, but remember that you will have to fill and repaint holes and recesses left by the original door hinges and handle. Doors are fairly heavy, so you will probably need someone to help you with the job of rehanging.

## TOOLS AND EQUIPMENT

**New door hinges** may be necessary if the old ones are in poor condition. Ordinary butt hinges are usually used for internal doors, but rising butt hinges are useful if, for example, the door has to clear fitted carpet. They're available for left or right-hand opening doors (see overleaf).

**Screwdrivers** For paint-jammed screws, use one with a large ball handle which gives a good grip. Or use a ratchet screwdriver – this is more expensive than an ordinary one but is easier to use as it can be adjusted to make half turns and you don't have to change your grip.

**A marking gauge** – a wooden rod with a moveable block that can be set at any point on it, and a pin to mark a cutting line – is useful for marking out recesses before cutting.

**Bevel-edged chisels** for cutting recesses: the most useful sizes range from 6mm to 25mm. A mallet is normally used for tapping the end of the chisel, or you can use a hammer.

*A smart appearance*
*Age and constant opening and closing take their toll on most doors. So, while a fresh coat of paint – or stripping and polishing – will work wonders on a shabby surface, make sure that any repairs are tackled first.*

*Here, the door, frame, and skirtings are picked out in a deep aqua-coloured gloss paint to tone in with the two different wallpapers used in the bathroom and hallway.*

## REHANGING A DOOR

Reverse a door by swapping the hinges and handle to the opposite side. Don't try to alter its position in the frame – if the door or the frame is at all out of square, or if the door has been adjusted in the past, it will not fit.

A door that fits well in its frame should have a 2 to 3mm clearance at top and sides and a sufficient gap at the bottom for it to clear the floor.

**1 Support the door** ▷
Open the door so that the hinges are fully exposed and drive a couple of small wood wedges underneath to take the weight of it.

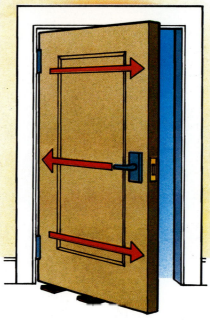

**2 Undo hinge screws on frame**
Scrape away any old paint from around the screw heads and loosen the screws that hold the hinges to the door frame. Remove all but one screw from each hinge, then take off the bottom hinge first, otherwise the door could fall on top of you. Remove the top hinge, and kick the wedges to one side to release the door.

**If hinges are stuck** If a screw is difficult to turn, place the tip of an old screwdriver in the slot and give it a sharp blow with a hammer to jar the screw – repeat until you can turn the screw easily.

If a hinge is paint-bound, prise it free with an old chisel.

**3 Remove the hinges**
Prop the door up against the wall. Remove the handle and any other door furniture, and store these in a safe place until you need them again.

Then stand the door on its side and take off the hinges. If the hinges are in good condition, soak them in paint stripper and re-use. Fill the old hinge recesses and screw holes in the frame and door with wood filler.

**4 Mark position of new hinges** ▷
Prop door in frame, and tap the wedges in underneath until they hold the door in the correct position. Using a pencil, mark the top and bottom edges of the new hinge positions on to both door and frame, opposite where the old hinges were.

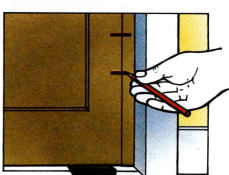

**5 Outline hinges** ▷
**on door**
Lay the door on its side. Place an open hinge on the edge of the door – inside the pencil marks, and with the knuckle projecting over the edge – and outline the flap with a pencil or knife.

Set a marking gauge to the thickness of the hinge flap and mark the depth of the hinge recess on to the door face.

**6 Cut recesses in door** ▷
Use a chisel and mallet to cut hinge recesses in the door. Score round the pencil outline with the tip of the chisel, make a series of shallow cuts across the grain, then pare out the waste down to the previously marked depth.

Position hinges and check that they lie flush with the timber. Mark screw holes through flaps, drill pilot holes and fix the hinges securely in place.

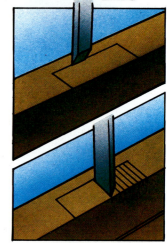

**7 Cut recesses in frame**
Wedge the door in the frame, this time in the open position.

Line up the free hinge flaps with the marks on the frame, making sure that the knuckles are parallel to it. Outline the flaps with a pencil or knife, remove the door and cut new recesses as in Step 6.

**8 Hang the door**
Wedge the door back in position, fit the top hinge into the recess in the frame and fix with one central screw. Repeat with the bottom hinge. Remove wedges and check that the door opens and closes properly.

If it catches the frame, you've probably cut the hinge recesses too deep or too shallow – either make the recesses deeper or fill them with pieces of thin card. When the door fits perfectly, fix the remaining screws.

## BRIGHT IDEA

### RISING BUTT HINGES

These allow a door to lift as it opens, and to be removed without taking off the hinges. The hinge is in two parts: one flap with a pin goes on the frame; another with a knuckle goes on the door and slides over the pin.

It's fixed in much the same way as an ordinary butt hinge (above), but first plane a shallow angle on the top edge of the door, hinge side, so that it can easily clear the door frame as it rises.

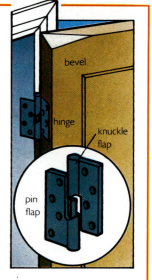

## CHECK YOUR NEEDS
**For rehanging a door:**
- ☐ Wood wedges
- ☐ Screwdrivers
- ☐ Paint stripper (optional)
- ☐ New hinges (optional)
- ☐ New screws
- ☐ Wood filler
- ☐ Steel rule and pencil
- ☐ Marking gauge
- ☐ Broad chisel
- ☐ Narrow chisel
- ☐ Mallet
- ☐ Hammer
- ☐ Bradawl
- ☐ Brace or drill and bit

**For general maintenance:**
- ☐ General-purpose oil
- ☐ Graphite powder – for locks
- ☐ Wooden dowels or plugging compound for screw holes
- ☐ Glasspaper, coarse and fine
- ☐ Carbon paper
- ☐ Thin cardboard or card

### FITTING A DOOR HANDLE

If you are rehanging a door – or even redecorating a room in a new style – this is a good opportunity to replace door fittings that are past their best with a new set. Use traditional china or brass knobs for panelled doors, or brightly coloured plastic lever handles for super-modern style.

Whatever the style of handle, the fitting procedure is much the same, but follow manufacturer's instructions as to size and positioning of fixing holes.

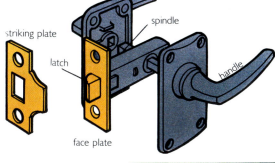

**1 Mark latch and spindle ▷**
Decide how high you want the handle and mark this height on to the two faces of the door.

Mark position of hole for latch on to centre of door edge. Then hold the latch against one side of the door, allowing for recess of latch face plate on door edge, and mark position of hole for spindle. Repeat on the other side of the door.

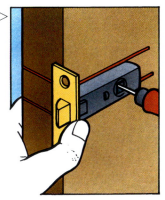

**2 Drill holes ▷**
Using a brace or drill and bit, bore a large hole into the edge of the door to take the latch.

Then bore a smaller hole for the spindle, drilling from both sides of the door to stop the bit from breaking through the wood and perhaps damaging the face of the door.

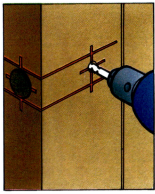

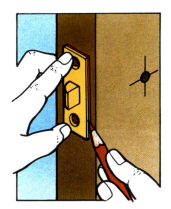

**3 Mark face plate △**
Insert the latch into the hole in the door edge and pencil around the face plate.

Remove the latch and, using a chisel and mallet, cut out a shallow recess so that the face plate lies flush with the door edge. Mark the screw hole positions and drill pilot holes; fit latch and screw plate into position.

**4 Fit the handle △**
Push the spindle into the hole in the face of the door and through the latch.

Fit the handles on to the spindle on both sides of the door, making sure that the vertical edge of the handle plate is parallel to the edge of the door. Mark positions of screw holes with a pencil, drill pilot holes and screw them in place.

**5 Mark striking plate △**
Close door against edge of frame, and use a pencil to mark the position for the striking plate on to the frame.

Measure the distance the latch face is set back from the door face; transfer this measurement to the frame so that the striking plate and latch line up. With plate in position, mark round it with a pencil or knife.

**6 Fit striking plate △**
Chisel out a deep hole to take the latch, and make a shallower recess for the plate so that it lies flush with the frame.

Mark screw hole positions on to the frame through the plate. Drill pilot holes, screw the plate in place, and check that the door closes properly.

## CURING DOOR FAULTS

Doors get plenty of hard wear, and over the years a door and its frame may develop irritating defects. Below are some common problems that can be easily solved.

### The door squeaks
A door that squeaks when opened and closed needs its hinges oiled. Use general-purpose oil – apply sparingly, and mop up surplus with an old rag.

Oil also works wonders for bolts and stiff handles, but do not oil locks – puff in graphite powder instead.

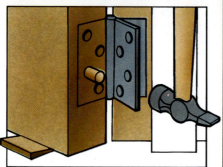

### The hinges are loose △
Hinges often work loose over time as a result of general wear and tear. Re-secure by tightening up loose screws and replacing missing ones.

Use slightly longer or thicker screws to replace any that will not tighten. If the screw holes are badly enlarged, hammer small pieces of wooden dowel into the holes, or fill the holes with plugging compound before replacing the screws.

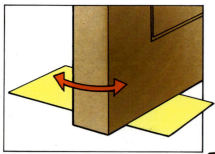

### The door catches on the floor △
If the door catches on an uneven floor when opened, first locate the problem places. Put a piece of coarse glasspaper over them and pull the door back and forth over the glasspaper a few times to remove a little wood. If possible, level out any high spots in the floor too: nail down loose floorboards and smooth the surface, and relay lifted tiles.

If the door makes a mark in a wide arc as it opens over the floor-covering, fit rising butt hinges (see page 22) or plane the bottom edge of the door – see above.

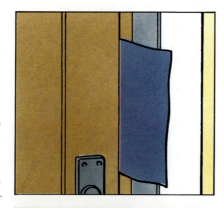

### The door sticks △
Sometimes a door sticks on the frame or on the floor because of a build up of paint, or because the wood has swollen due to temperature changes.

Find out where it is sticking by putting pieces of carbon paper between the door and the frame to mark the spot. Then use a plane to remove just enough paint or wood off the door edge to allow it to close easily, working from the corners into the centre of the door to avoid splitting the wood. You may have to remove the door first.

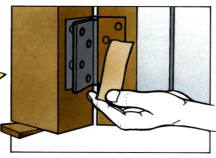

### The door won't close △
If a door sticks on the hinge side of the frame before it is fully closed, it usually means the hinges have been set too deep in the door or frame.

Support the door on wedges. Unscrew one hinge at a time and insert a piece of thin card or cardboard into the recess behind the hinge. Then refix screws, making sure that they fit flush with the hinge flaps. If the door still sticks, put another piece of cardboard in each recess.

### The door rattles
If a door rattles, the wood may have shrunk so that the door no longer sits tightly against the door stop inside the frame.

The simplest remedy is to move the striking plate on the frame slightly in towards the door stop.

**1 Mark the frame △**
Mark where door meets frame when closed. Hold latch in, push door against stop; mark frame again.

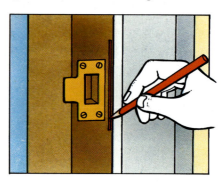

**2 Measure up △**
Measure between the two pencil points, and mark this distance behind the striking plate by drawing a vertical line parallel with its back edge.

**3 Remove the striking plate**
Unscrew the plate. Move it up to the pencil line and mark around it with a pencil or knife. Using a chisel and mallet, cut out a shallow recess to take the plate, and make a deeper hole to take the latch.

**4 Replace the striking plate**
Screw the striking plate in position and check that the door closes properly. For a neat finish, fill the gap left at the front of the plate with wood filler and paint over.

# RENOVATING CUPBOARD DOORS

If your cupboards are looking sad, some simple repairs and a facelift will give them a new lease of life.

Cupboards have been popular pieces of furniture for centuries as an essential way of providing storage for the hundreds of possessions in the average home. They come in all sorts of styles, shapes and sizes, but the basic design – a box with one or more doors on the front – remains the same whether the piece is ancient or modern, wall-hung or freestanding. The materials from which they are made may be natural timber or a man-made board, and the door style may be elaborate – miniature versions of traditional room doors, with a frame and inset panels – or plain – perhaps just a sheet of veneered or plastic-faced board.

Because cupboards are worked so hard, they tend to show their age as the years go by, and the part that suffers the most is the door itself. It's opened and closed regularly (and sometimes none too gently), so the handles, hinges and catches wear and become loose or damaged. Worse still, the actual appearance of the door goes into a steady decline, with knocks, scratches and stains marring the finish.

If your cupboards are going downhill fast, you have three choices: you can buy new cupboards; you can fit replacement doors but keep the existing carcases; or you can refurbish the doors, adjusting or replacing worn hardware so they work properly again and perhaps re-facing the door or adding some decorative trims to cheer it up. The last course of action is by far the most economical and least drastic.

## IMPROVING THE ACTION

Whatever type of cupboard doors you have, fixing any faults in the hardware – hinges, handles and catches – should be your first step. There is nothing more annoying than a door that won't open or close easily, or is sagging on its hinges, or has a handle that keeps coming away in your hand. Hinges can be adjusted so the door closes smoothly and squarely, or can be replaced if they're worn or damaged. Similarly, catches that don't engage can be repositioned, and old, inefficient ones can be replaced with modern easy-action types featuring ball, roller, or magnetic action. Lastly, new handles can be fitted – one of the best ways of brightening up a tired old door.

## IMPROVING THE LOOKS

The way you go about giving your doors a facelift depends on what type they are. Doors with a solid timber frame and inset timber or glass panels will probably benefit from being thoroughly cleaned; it may be better to strip them right back to bare wood and give them a new finish. At the same time, you can attend to any dents, splits, or stains. Plain doors, with veneer or a plastic surface over chipboard or blockboard, can also be cleaned down and repainted, or given a brand new surface with stick-on facing panels in hard-wearing plastic laminate. You can also add decorative edge trims, or even surface beading, to give the doors a brand new look.

*Cupboard love*
*Flush cupboard doors (and drawers) look particularly smart with a beading trim – here, matching beading has been used to decorate plain sections of wall as well. The effect is emphasized by drag painting the centre of the panel.*

### CHECK YOUR NEEDS
- Screwdrivers (several sizes, for slotted and cross-head screws)
- Bradawl
- Electric drill and twist drills
- Chisel and mallet
- Craft knife
- Abrasive paper or sanding block
- Plough plane, router or shaping attachment (for inset edge trims)
- Replacement hinges, catches, handles, plus fixing screws
- New door skin plus adhesive
- Door edge and face trims plus adhesive or panel pins

## MAKING DOORS FIT
If your cupboard doors don't close properly, the cause may be a simple build-up of paint or varnish on the door or frame, warping of the door itself, or a problem with the hinges or catch.

**1 Ease edges of door ▷**
Remove built-up layers of paint or varnish from edges that stick, either by sanding them or by stripping them completely back to bare wood, ready for refinishing. With doors that close within a frame, try to aim for about 2mm clearance all round.

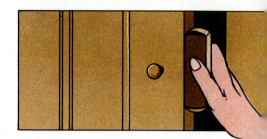

**2 Straighten warped doors ▷**
Correct a warped frame-and-panel door by removing it and cramping it flat. Use G-cramps to cramp it to a portable or solid workbench, or cramp it to lengths of timber the width of the door if it is too large for a work bench. Insert thin packing pieces as you cramp the door up to help counteract the warp.

There is not much you can do to correct warping in flush doors with man-made cores: it's easier to make and fit a new door. Cramping may help to straighten plywood doors. Remember that doors faced with plastic laminate must have a balancing veneer of the same thickness on the inner face; if this is not fitted, the door will warp again. You can use cheap plain laminate unless you want both sides to match.

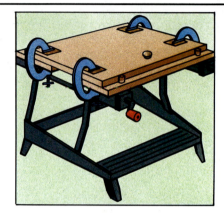

**3 Check the hinges**
Check that the screws holding the hinges and catch are secure, tightening any that have worked loose. If the threads will no longer bite, use a slightly longer or fatter screw, but check first that it isn't so long that it will go right through the wood, or so fat that it won't pass through the fixing hole in the hinge or catch itself.

Where physical damage has actually wrenched the screws out completely, either drill out the damaged holes and glue in a matching length of dowel to provide a firm fixing again, or else reposition the hinges so you can use new screw holes. If the hinges are modern concealed types, it may be possible to adjust them to improve the fit of the door – see opposite.

## REPLACING CATCHES
Fitting a new catch is often the quickest way of curing a door that either refuses to open when you want it to, or won't stay closed. The commonest types for cupboards use magnets, rollers, or ball bearings. Both surface-mounted and inset or flush-fitting types are available.

**2 Fit catch and plate ▷**
Mount the catch body on the cabinet or door, as recommended in the fitting instructions. With surface-mounted types, check that you fit it the right distance from the cabinet or door edge; with magnetic types, the magnet must be able to make physical contact with the striking plate; ball and roller types must be set back slightly to allow the striking plate to engage properly.

With flush-fitting types, the catch body and striking plate can be fitted either way round, although ball types can only be used on doors closing within a frame. Both involve drilling a blind hole to accept the catch body; the keeper or striking plate is surface-mounted with small screws or pins.

**1 Decide where to fit the catch**
Start by removing the old catch. Make good any holes, then decide on the best fixing position for the new catch; generally you can fit it to the side, base, or top of the cupboard, with the striking plate or keeper attached to the door itself. Some roller catches have to be fitted to the door, with the striking plate on the cupboard.

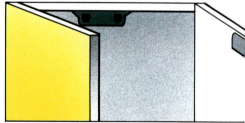

△ Single magnetic catch.
▽ Roller catch mounted inside door.

△ Double magnetic touch catch.
▽ Ball catch set into door frame.

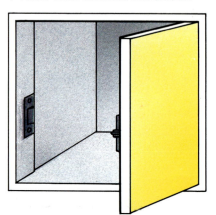

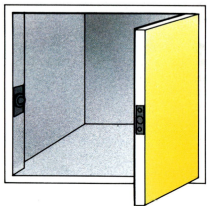

## ADJUSTING HINGES

Many modern cupboards, especially fitted kitchen and bedroom units, have concealed hinges that allow precise adjustment of the door action. The hinge itself is actually in two parts, with a baseplate attached to the sides of the cupboard and the hinge body recessed into a round hole milled in the inner face of the door.

**1** *Adjusting to left and right*
To move the door slightly to the left or right, adjust the screw on the baseplate nearest to the front edge of the cupboard. This moves the hinge arm in a horizontal plane, towards or away from the cupboard side, and so moves the door sideways. You may need to adjust the other hinge(s) too.

**2** *Adjusting distance from carcase*
To move the door closer to or further away from the carcase, loosen the screw holding the hinge arm to the baseplate. Then slide the hinge arm into or out of the cupboard as required, and tighten up the fixing screw again.

**3** *Adjusting up and down*
Some hinges allow the door position to be adjusted up and down as well, and this is carried out by adjusting the screw beside one of the baseplate fixing screws. Slacken these off slightly first, then make the height adjustment and tighten the fixing screws up again.

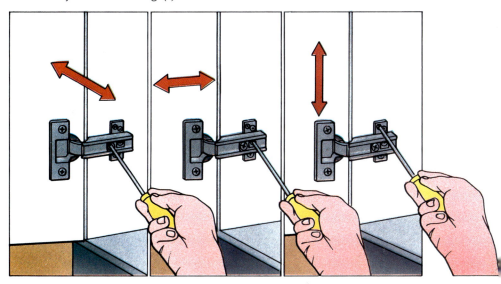

## RESURFACING DOORS

You can give flush cupboard doors a new lease of life by giving them a fresh outer face. You can do this yourself using paint or wallpaper (see Bright Idea, at right), but for modern kitchen cupboard doors one of the easiest methods is to use special peel-and-stick plastic laminate which is available in standard door widths and a range of colours.

**1** *Start at the top ▷*
The panel should be a centimetre or so larger all round than the door. It is easier to handle if it is trimmed to this size. Clean the door surface thoroughly. Then peel a couple of centimetres of backing paper away from one end of the panel and position the top edge of the panel at the top of the door, aligning it to leave a small trim allowance.

**2** *Peel and smooth panel ▷*
Gradually peel off a little more of the backing paper, and smooth the panel down into place with a dry sponge or cloth pad to ensure good adhesion and eliminate any air bubbles.

**3** *Trim edges ▷*
Peel off the last of the backing paper and rub down the panel once again. Then use a sharp knife to trim all round the edges of the panel, flush with the door edges. Cut with the right side facing you. Cut strips to finish edges if necessary.

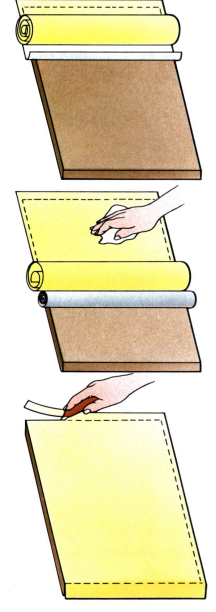

## BRIGHT IDEA

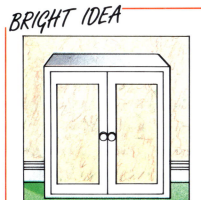

**Paper it over** You can give cupboard doors a quick and inexpensive facelift by wallpapering them – perhaps to match an existing colour scheme. Any wallcovering can be used within reason, although in kitchens and bathrooms it's a good idea to use a washable type. Or varnish over the wallpaper.

With panelled doors, simply cut the wallpaper to fit each panel and stick it in place with wallpaper paste. Wash down the door surface first, then sand it lightly. With flush doors, it's best to apply the paper, cutting it slightly larger than the finished panel area, and then to pin on a slim decorative beading so it covers the edges.

## ADDING TRIMS

With plain flush cupboard doors it's usually the edges that get damaged. If they are made of plastic-faced chipboard the edging strips can be knocked off completely. These can then be replaced with peel-and-stick edging strips, or iron-on edging, which comes in rolls.

To make a plain wooden door more interesting, you can add wooden beading – either round the very edge of the door, or set in a few centimetres from the edge to create decorative panels to imitate traditional panelled doors.

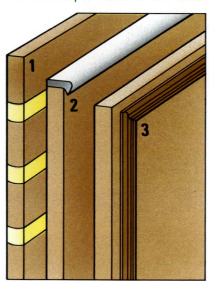

**1 Using stick-on trims ▷**
Cut the pieces to length, peel off backing and stick in place. If the strip is not self-adhesive, use the recommended adhesive, holding the trims in place with lengths of strong tape until the adhesive has dried. Wipe off any excess adhesive that oozes out.

**2 Adding wooden edge trims ▷**
First check that there is room to add a trim. If the door is too tight, you may be able to plane a few millimetres off the edge to accommodate the beading. Otherwise, resort to laminate or veneer trims (see above). Choose a beading with a recess deep enough for the door. Glue and pin in place.

**3 Adding surface-mounted trims ◁**
Moulded beading can be added round the edge of flush doors to give them a more sophisticated look. It can also be added set in about 10cm from the edge of the door, to imitate traditional-style panels. Check that the beading does not catch on the door or the frame before fixing. Measure and cut the beading carefully, mitring the corners (see page 19). Apply glue to the beading, then pin in place. Punch the heads of the panel pins below the surface, and fill with the appropriate filler.

---

## CHANGING DOOR FURNITURE

When you've finished restoring your cupboard doors to good health, fitting new knobs or handles adds the finishing touch. There is a huge range of fittings available in both period and modern styles; all you have to do is decide which type to go for.

**1 Prepare the door**
Remove the old handles, and make good old fixing holes with wood stopper. If possible, choose new handles that will conceal the old screw holes. If you are fitting handles or knobs that are secured by small bolts or screws driven through the door from behind, you may be able to use the existing fixing holes. Check first.

**2 Fit new handles**
Fit the new handles, using adhesive, screws, or pins as appropriate. Check that bar handles are level, and that rows of knobs or handles on a run of cupboards are all at the same height.

◁ **Moulded to suit**
Most DIY stores stock a good range of hardwood mouldings which can be used to trim cupboard doors: here the selection includes astragal and embossed moulding.

# REPLACING THE WOODWORK

Replacing skirtings, architrave and other woodwork can make all the difference to the character of a room.

Wood mouldings are widely used in the home for both decorative and practical purposes. The most common are skirting boards around the foot of walls, and architraves round door and window openings. Older houses may have a chair rail fixed to the wall at roughly waist level, and also a picture rail about three-quarters of the way up the wall.

Woodwork can make a big difference to the character and appearance of a room, and is often worth reinstating, if the original features are missing – or replacing, if they have been damaged.

This is fairly easy to do as the woodwork is not part of the house's structure. However, as cutting accurate joints – particularly in large, ornately-shaped mouldings such as skirting – is not always so straightforward, it is sensible to choose plain, small-section mouldings for your first attempts. If mouldings are just loose, they can be nailed or screwed back in place.

## CHOOSING TIMBER MOULDINGS

Any good timber merchant carries a wide choice of timber mouldings in a range of sizes and fancy profiles. They are available in soft and hardwoods, but the latter are more expensive.

Softwood mouldings are usually primed and painted or stained and varnished; hardwood mouldings are normally just varnished. It is generally easier to sand the mouldings so that they're ready for decorating before cutting and fixing.

**Skirting boards** are generally between 100 and 175mm high, and 19 or 25mm thick. They can be plain, or have a decorative shape along the top edge – see overleaf.

**Architraves** are usually 75 or 100mm wide, although wider mouldings were quite common in Victorian times. Profiles on architraves are similar to those found on skirting boards.

**Chair rails** carry a decorative moulding on both edges, with a flat section in between. They are between 38 and 62mm high, and project by 25mm.

**Picture rails** have a deep groove running along the top edge in which picture hooks can be fixed. Most are about 38mm high, and project by up to 25mm.

## TOOLS AND EQUIPMENT

**A bench hook** is a small piece of wood, with a batten along its top at one end, and another along its underside at the opposite end. It is a simple and useful tool for holding work secure while sawing, and can be easily hooked on the edge of a work-bench, if you have one, or a work table.

**A tenon saw** is used for making straight cuts – freehand or with a mitre box.

**A coping saw**, which takes very fine blades, is the best tool for cutting out the curved shapes of scribed profiles.

**A mitre box** is an essential aid for making accurate 45° cuts for mitred joints. It can, however, be used only with mouldings up to about 100mm high as the base of the box must be wide enough for the moulding to lie flat.

**A powered jig saw or circular saw** with an adjustable soleplate can be used to cut accurate mitres in skirting that is too wide for a mitre box.

**Fixing nails** Use masonry nails for fixing mouldings to masonry, and oval wire nails if fixing to timber. Use panel pins for reinforcing mitred joints.

### Bold lines
*Skirting, chair rail and architrave are picked out in bright yellow for a cheerful, modern look. The chair rail makes an attractive visual break between two contrasting wallpapers.*

## MOULDING PROFILES
Below are some of the most common shapes for mouldings.

### Skirting boards

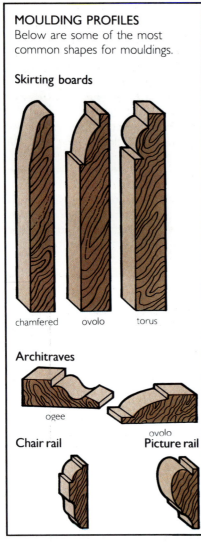

chamfered   ovolo   torus

### Architraves

ogee

ovolo

Chair rail          Picture rail

## CHECK YOUR NEEDS
**For removing old trim:**
- ☐ Bolster or crowbar
- ☐ Old wood chisel
- ☐ Claw hammer
- ☐ Block of scrap wood
- ☐ Cold chisel
- ☐ Craft knife
- ☐ Nail punch
- ☐ Hacksaw

**For fixing new trim:**
- ☐ New mouldings
- ☐ Steel rule and pencil
- ☐ Try square for 90° cuts
- ☐ Mitre box, combination square or set square for 45° cuts OR powered jig or circular saw
- ☐ Bench hook
- ☐ Tenon saw
- ☐ Coping saw
- ☐ Spirit level
- ☐ Drill and bit
- ☐ Fixing nails
- ☐ Nail punch and hammer
- ☐ Wood filler
- ☐ All-purpose filler for small holes, plaster for large holes

## FIXING NEW SKIRTING
How you fix new skirting depends on what is behind the old skirting.

In older houses, the plaster often finishes at skirting-board level (right) and the boards are nailed to timber 'grounds' – short wooden battens of the same thickness as the plaster, nailed to the masonry at about one metre intervals round the room. In more modern houses, the plaster usually extends to the floor (far right) and boards are nailed through into masonry behind. On hollow walls, boards are fixed with nails driven into the timber studs.

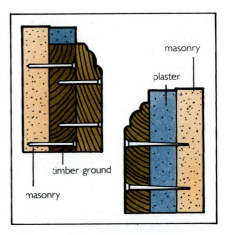

**1 Remove the old skirting ▷**
Skirting is usually nailed in place but look out for screws. To remove the old skirting, start at a corner where the boards overlap – an external corner if there is one, an internal one otherwise – and use a hammer and bolster to lever it off. If the plaster overlaps the top edge of boards, drive the bolster in horizontally to make a clean break. Then drive it downwards and carefully lever the board away from the wall. As soon as there is a gap between wall and skirting, place a block of scrap wood behind the bolster to protect the wall.

If the fixing nails are visible, it may be quicker to free the skirting by driving the nails right through the boards into the wall with a hammer and nail punch. Once the boards have been lifted away, prise out the nails or cut them off with a cold chisel and hammer.

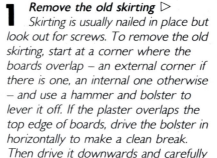

**Check timber grounds** If these are split or riddled with woodworm, prise them off. Cut new grounds from wooden battens of the correct thickness, soak them overnight in wood preservative and leave them to dry. Then drill pilot holes in new grounds, and fix in place with masonry nails.

**2 Plan ahead ▷**
Fix boards in the order shown so that any slight gaps in joints won't be too visible. Wherever possible, fit a single length of board on each wall. If joins cannot be avoided, site them near an inconspicuous corner – where timber grounds exist, position joins over these.

For neatness and a good fit, external corners are mitred; at internal corners, one board is scribed with the profile of the adjacent board. Try to arrange the boards so that one end is left plain and fits into an internal corner of the room.

**3 Measure and cut the first board**
Measure the length of the wall against which the first board will fit, and allow about 50mm extra for ends to be scribed or mitred – see opposite. Use a tenon saw to cut the board.

If one end is to be scribed to fit into an internal corner, do this first. Then prepare a mitred end for an external corner, or mark up a straight cut with a try square. Make sure that the board is cut to the correct length – if it is to be butt-jointed, subtract the thickness of the board from the wall measurement.

**4 Fix the board**
Check that the board fits the wall, then drill pilot holes for the fixing nails in the flat surface of the board. Where you position the fixings depends on what is behind the skirting. If there are timber grounds, make sure that you drive the nails into these by marking their position on to the right side of the skirting. If plaster extends to floor level, nail directly on to this; on hollow walls, nail into the timber frame.

If possible, get someone to hold the board in place while you are working.

**5 Fix remaining boards**
Continue round the room, measuring and cutting each board after fixing the adjacent one in position. At external corners, drive light nails or panel pins through the mitred joints.

Punch in the nail heads with a hammer and nail punch and cover them with wood filler. Then make good any damage to the plasterwork: fill small cracks and holes with all-purpose filler, larger holes with plaster. Finally, paint or varnish the new skirting.

## DEALING WITH CORNERS
On internal corners, one board must be cut to match the profile of the board at right angles to it. External corners are always mitred.

### Internal corners ▷
Fit a board with a straight cut end into the corner first. Using an offcut of skirting, trace the shape of the moulding on to the board that is to be fitted against it. Cut the board carefully along the line with a coping saw, and fit it against the board on the adjacent wall.

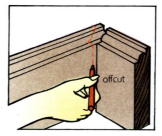

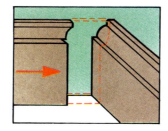

### External corners
If you have a jig saw or circular saw, use it with its soleplate set to a 45° angle to cut a mitre across the end of the board.

If you have to do this by hand, use a combination square or set square to mark the board with the angle at a fraction over 45° so that, when the two halves of the mitre are put together, any gap will be on the inside of the joint rather than on the outside. Then cut the mitred end very carefully with a tenon saw.

## FITTING NEW ARCHITRAVE
Architraves are set slightly away from the edge of the door or window frame, and neatly cover the join with the surrounding wall finish.

They are usually fixed to the frame of the door or window with oval wire nails that are driven through the moulding's inner edge.

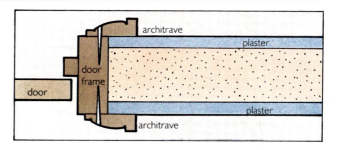

**1 Remove old architrave**
Start by prising off the vertical sections of the architrave (the uprights) with a hammer and bolster. Work from the door edge of the architrave to avoid excessive damage to the wall surface, and look out for nails securing the mitred top corners together.

Carefully prise off the top section of the architrave (the head section) in the same way. Then use a claw hammer to lever out any fixing nails that have gone through the architrave into the door frame.

**2 Cut new uprights ▷**
Measure the height of the door frame and cut two new pieces of moulding for the uprights slightly longer than necessary for mitring.

Position one upright against the door frame, butting the bottom end against the floor and skirting board. At the top end, carefully mark off the height of the opening on the inner edge of the upright – this will be the inside edge of the mitred cut. Then use a mitre box (see overleaf) to cut the top end at a 45° angle. Repeat with the other upright.

**3 Fix uprights in position**
Position each of the two uprights against the door frame, parallel with its inner edge and away from it by about 6mm; butt the bottom ends against the floor and skirting. Lightly nail in place through the inner edge of the architrave into the door frame – don't drive the nails fully home at this stage in case you need to reposition the uprights.

**4 Cut the head section ▷**
Measure across the top of the door opening, and cut a piece of moulding for the head section slightly overlength to allow for mitring the ends. Hold the moulding upside down across the tops of the uprights, and mark off both ends.

Cut one mitre. Then hold the head section in place, and check the position of the other mitre before cutting it.

**5 Fix the head section ▷**
Check that the head section fits exactly, and adjust if necessary – by adjusting the positions of the uprights slightly or planing the mitres carefully if they do not meet exactly.

Then nail all three pieces firmly in position, and drive pins into the outside edge of each mitred join to prevent them from opening up.

## USING A MITRE BOX

The only way to get moulded pieces of wood to meet properly in a right angle is to make a mitre joint by cutting the joining ends at 45°. With small-section mouldings – such as architrave, dado and picture rails – the best way to do this is with a mitre box.

Hold the mitre box steady, using a bench hook if you have one. Place the moulding in the box – lay architrave flat in the bottom, face up; hold a dado or picture rail vertically against the wall of the box, facing away from you. Place a flat piece of scrap wood under the moulding so that you can saw right through into the scrap and get a clean cut. Position your tenon saw at an angle between corresponding slots on opposite sides of the box, making sure that the cut slopes the correct way. Hold the moulding firm and cut.

If you don't have a mitre box, use a combination square or set square to mark the 45° cutting line, then cut very carefully with a tenon saw.

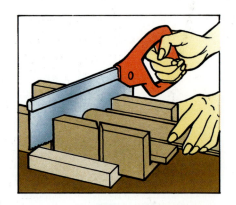

## FIXING DADO AND PICTURE RAILS

Dado and picture rails are usually fixed on top of plaster, and should not be too difficult to prise off the wall.

In older houses, however, you may find that they were positioned before the walls were plastered so that the plaster overlaps the edges. If this is the case, be prepared for some fairly extensive repair after removing them, as you're likely to dislodge quite a bit of plaster.

**1 Remove the old rail ▷**
Starting roughly in the centre of the rail, insert the blade of an old wood chisel between the rail and wall and carefully prise it away. If it snaps at the positions of the fixing nails, prise the nails out later using a claw hammer, with a piece of scrap wood behind the hammer to protect the plaster. If the nails won't budge, use a hacksaw to saw them flush with the wall.

If you can't get a chisel behind the rail, it was probably fixed before plastering. To minimize damage, run a craft knife along both edges of the rail to break the bond with the plaster. Split the rail into sections with a chisel and lever off. Repair any damage to the wall with filler or new plaster.

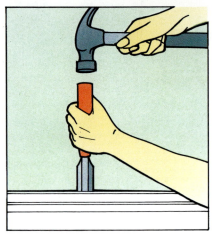

**2 Draw a horizontal guideline ▷**
Measure the distance up from the top of the skirting board (for a dado rail) or down from the ceiling (for a picture rail), and mark where the rail is to be fixed at several points. Then, using a spirit level, draw a horizontal line on the wall right round the room. Make sure that your start and finish points coincide, and adjust if necessary.

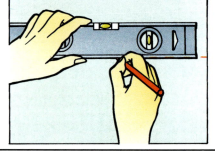

**3 Measure and cut the first rail**
As with skirtings (see pages 30-31), internal angles are scribed, and external angles are mitred. Fit straight cut ends against windows and doors.

Measure the length of the wall against which the first rail will fit and cut the rail about 50mm overlong. Then prepare the ends as necessary, making sure that the rail is exactly to length.

**4 Fix the rail in place**
Check the rail for fit, then drill pilot holes and fix it in place with slim masonry pins at 600mm intervals.

If possible, get someone to hold the rail in place against the pencil guide line while you drive in the pins. To stop the rail from wandering off line, drive a pin in at one end, then fix the other end before driving in the intermediate pins.

**5 Fix the remaining rails ▷**
Work round the room, measuring and cutting each rail after the adjacent one has been fixed in position.

Punch in the fixing nails to just below the surface of the wood with a hammer and nail punch, and fill the holes with wood filler. Fill any small gaps between rail and wall with filler, and finally decorate the rails with paint or varnish.

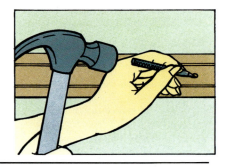

## BRIGHT IDEA

### DECORATING WOOD TRIMS

Paint techniques, such as dragging and graining, are particularly effective on woodwork and more interesting than plain paint or varnish. Here, for example, a blue dragged finish highlights the horizontal direction of the wood grain and the printed border along the top of the skirting. For a really neat finish with these techniques, it is generally easier to paint mouldings after cutting them to size but before fixing them in place.

# CLADDING WALLS WITH TIMBER

Wooden tongued-and-grooved cladding gives to any room a warmth and richness that few other materials can offer.

Wooden panelling of one sort or another has been a popular way of decorating interior walls for centuries. It is good-looking, hardwearing and warm to the touch, and can be crafted and finished in several different ways.

One of the easiest panelled effects to install is tongued-and-grooved (t-and-g) cladding. Softwood, including knotty pine, is an obvious choice, but other more exotic woods such as cedar, mahogany, ramin and meranti can be used instead. A visit to a good timber merchant will reveal the choice available, and if you want something a little unusual he may be able to prepare a particular wood specially for you.

Apart from its looks, cladding has other advantages. For a start, it's the perfect cover-up for walls with defective (or missing) plaster. It is warm to the touch, so helps to cut down condensation, and if insulation is fitted behind it the result is a much warmer room – a particular boon in properties with solid walls which are difficult to insulate.

It also helps to reduce noise transmission between rooms. The only drawback is that the room is made slightly smaller as a result, and some repositioning of fittings such as wall lights, switches and power points may be required.

It is not necessary to clad complete rooms – or even complete walls: you can panel below the dado rail height, or up to the height of a picture rail (or plate shelf).

**Fixing cladding** The boards are usually fixed to the walls by nailing them to a network of sawn timber battens. For vertical cladding, these are fixed at floor and ceiling (or dado rail/picture rail) level and horizontally at intervals of about 600mm (2ft) in between, while for horizontal cladding the intermediate battens are fixed vertically. If insulation is to be incorporated (see overleaf), this is placed between the battens before the boards are fixed in place.

**Finishes** Once the boards have been fixed, the surface can be finished with paint (knot, prime and undercoat first), varnish, stain or polish, according to the final effect you want to achieve.

*Freshly clad*
*Tongued-and-grooved boards take on a fresh country look in this living room. A soft blue painted finish is a restful contrast to the cottagey wallpaper. Cladding below the dado rail is a clever way of disguising a poor plaster finish – where a new damp proof course has been installed, for instance. To add to the country look, a combination of 110- and 150mm-wide boards have been used.*

## SHAPES AND SIZES

Cladding of this sort is usually sold in the form of planks 100 to 150mm (4 to 6in) wide and 12 to 19mm (½ to ¾in) thick, in lengths of 2.4 to 3m (8 to 10ft). One edge of each board has a tongue machined along it, while the other has a mating groove; these allow adjacent boards to interlock without a gap being visible between them.

Cutting the tongue reduces the actual face width of the board by up to 6mm (¼in), a point worth remembering when you are estimating how many planks are necessary to cover a wall.

Plain t-and-g boards look rather like narrow floorboards when butted together, but the addition of chamfering along each face edge emphasizes the joint line and gives a more attractive overall effect. Such boards are usually described as tongued, grooved and vee-jointed (tgv in the timber merchant's jargon). You can also get tgv boards with a concave outer face, or with grooves in the surface to give reeded or piped effects (see right).

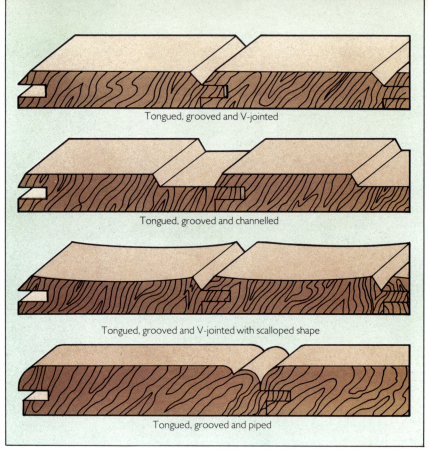

Tongued, grooved and V-jointed

Tongued, grooved and channelled

Tongued, grooved and V-jointed with scalloped shape

Tongued, grooved and piped

## PANELLING LIMITED AREAS

There is no need to feel you have to panel a whole room – or even a whole wall. Panelling up to dado rail height, panelling an alcove, or panelling a section of a wall where a feature (such as a fireplace) has been removed can be very effective.

*Panelling a chimney breast* ▷
*When fireplaces are removed it is difficult to get a good, even finish on the chimney breast, even if you call in a professional plasterer. There is no reason why you shouldn't panel over the bumps. There are no rules about how high you should take the panelling: you could just panel a fireplace shape, finishing it with a shelf, to look like a mantelshelf. Another suggestion, shown here, is to continue the panelling up the wall to picture-rail height, and add nosing at the top of the panelling or a wider shelf to take an arrangement of plates, or a collection of teapots.*

*Panelling the lower half of a room*
*You can panel the lower half of a room, to chair-rail height. Use a piece of hockey stick moulding or nosing to give a neat finish along the top edge. This is ideal for covering damaged plaster.*

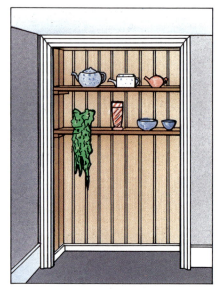

*Panelling an alcove △*
*If plasterwork in an alcove is crumbling, for example where cupboards or shelves have been removed, fit t-and-g to create a built-in dresser effect, with an architrave surround.*

## PREPARATION FOR CLADDING

**1** *Preliminary planning*
Cladding can be fixed over any existing wall surface or decoration, even to bare brickwork, so no formal preparation is needed. However, there is some preliminary planning to be done.

First, you have to decide on which way the cladding is to run, and whether to remove the existing skirting board. You can use this as the floor-level fixing ground if you wish, adding hardboard packing to its surface if it's thinner than the battening, but if it's an ornate type you may prefer to remove it so you can replace it when the cladding is in position. Prise it off carefully using a brick bolster or similar tool – see page 30 for more details.

Work out how many boards you will need, and make sure that if you start at one end of the wall with a full width board you don't end up with an awkwardly narrow space to fill at the far end.

**2** *Dealing with electrics*
Next, you will have to reposition any flush-mounted light switches and power points on the wall to be clad so that once you have finished the face plates can be mounted on the new cladding. If you don't have a thorough understanding of electrics, call in an electrician. Ask him to leave the power to the room disconnected and to leave the face plates off, ready for re-fitting over the new cladding.

**CHECK YOUR NEEDS**
- ☐ Tongued-and-grooved planks
- ☐ 50×25mm sawn softwood battens
- ☐ Hardboard for packing as needed
- ☐ 63mm masonry nails OR 63mm No 8 screws and wallplugs
- ☐ 25mm panel pins
- ☐ Edge mouldings
- ☐ Glasspaper and sanding block OR Electrical orbital sander and abrasives
- ☐ Paint, varnish or stain
- ☐ 25mm thick polystyrene insulation boards (optional)
- ☐ Retractable metal tape measure
- ☐ Spirit level
- ☐ Claw hammer OR Electric drill and masonry bit
- ☐ Screwdriver
- ☐ Tenon and coping saw
- ☐ Pencil and scribing block
- ☐ Pin hammer and nail punch
- ☐ Varnishing or painting equipment

## VERTICAL CLADDING

**1 Fix the battening ▷**
Start by fixing battens at the top and sides of the wall to be clad, and at floor level if you have removed the skirting. It's quickest to fix them with masonry nails at about 300mm intervals, but if the wall surface is very uneven it's better to use screws and wallplugs so you can add slips of hardboard as packing where necessary behind the battening. Avoid driving nails or screws in directly above or below switches and sockets, where cables may be buried; it's a good idea to use a small DIY metal detector to track down cable runs if you're not sure where they are.

**2 Intermediate battens ▷**
Add intermediate battens at about 600mm intervals across the wall, running horizontally for vertical cladding. Again, add slips of hardboard if the wall is at all uneven.
Finally, fix short battens round repositioned switch or socket mounting boxes; turn off the power while working and take care not to damage the buried cables as you do this.
If the wall contains a door or window opening in a reveal and this is to be clad too, add battens to the faces of the reveal as well.

**3 Fit the insulation**
If you plan to fit polystyrene insulation boards behind the t-and-g, it should be added next. Simply cut the 2440×1220mm sheets into strips to match the spaces between the battens and wedge them into place. Use adhesive tape to hold any that are a loose fit until you fix the cladding over them.

**4 Fix the first board ◁**
It's important that the boards are fixed to a true vertical (or horizontal). With vertical cladding, cut the first board to length and offer it up to one edge of the area to be clad with the grooved edge in the corner. Use a spirit level to ensure that it is vertical and pin it temporarily in place. Then scribe the profile of the side wall and its skirting board on to the face of the cladding with a scribing block and pencil (see page 72).

**5 Pin the board in place ▽**
Take the board down and use a coping saw to cut along the marked line. Then offer the board back into position, check the vertical again and nail it to the battens with panel pins driven at an angle through the exposed tongue close to the shoulder. Add extra pins level with each batten, driven through the face of the board, near the scribed edge, and punch the heads in just below the board surface. The holes will be filled later.

**6 Fix the other whole boards ▽**
Fix the second board by sliding its grooved edge over the tongue of the first board; note that this conceals the pins completely to give a concealed fixing. If the boards are a tight fit, use a scrap of t-and-g to protect the tongued edge while you knock each one in place. Then drive pins through its tongue as before. Repeat this process to fix all the other full-length boards to the battens. Leave the last length, which needs to be scribed to fit (see Step 8).

**7 Fix cladding round fittings ▽**
To fix cladding round a light switch or socket outlet, small cut-outs have to be made in the adjacent boards. After fixing the last whole board before the obstacle, hold the next one in place and mark the mounting box position on it. Make the cut-out with a coping saw and fix the length in place, nailing it to the battens round the box. Then offer up, mark, cut and fit the second length to frame the box. Re-fit the faceplate when decorating is complete.

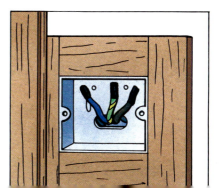

**8** *Coping with external corners* ▽
At window reveals, chimney breasts and other external corners you should aim to get a neat finish, without the groove or the tongue showing. After fitting the last full-width board, measure the distance left to be clad. Cut down the length of the tongued edge of the last board on the main wall surface so it protrudes beyond the battening by an amount equal to the thickness of the board. Then butt the grooved edge of the first board round the external corner up against this overlap, and fix the board in place. Add a decorative corner beading if you wish to conceal the join. See 'Finishing touches', below.

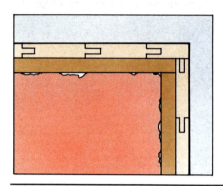

**9** *Internal corners* ▽
At internal corners, the last length must be scribed and cut down to width. Pin or hold it on top of the last whole board fitted, and use an offcut of cladding to scribe the wall profile on to the board. Cut along the scribed line, offer the board up into position and fix it to the battens with pins driven through the board face. If the adjoining wall is also being clad, simply butt the grooved edge of the first length to be fixed to this wall against the surface of the last, scribed board on the other wall. Fix in place close to the grooved edge by knocking pins straight through the board face and the tongue.

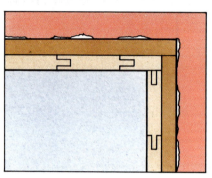

## FIXING HORIZONTAL CLADDING
**1** *Fix the battens*
Horizontal cladding has to be fixed to vertical battens. Fix the battens round the edge of the wall first, as for vertical cladding, then fix vertical battens every 600mm or so across the wall. Add hardboard packing and insulation if necessary in the same way as described for vertical cladding.

**2** *The first board*
The lowest board is the first board to be fitted. Scribing is usually unnecessary, since you will probably cover the wall/floor angle with a skirting board. Fit the board with the tongued edge at the top, using a spirit level to make sure that the board is level. Pin the board to the vertical battens through the tongue as before.

**3** *Add the remaining boards*
Continue fixing boards, working up to the ceiling. At the top, cut the tongued edge to fit neatly. You may need to scribe the top board to make a tidy angle with the ceiling if you are not going to cover the angle with coving.

## FINISHING TOUCHES
**1** *Neaten the edges* ▽
However carefully you work, the cut ends of the boards always look a little ragged. Neaten them off by adding slim quadrant or scotia beading at ceiling and wall edges, and replace the skirting board at floor level. Where cladding finishes on an external corner, pin a slim moulding to the edge of the last batten to hide it and the board edge. If the cladding doesn't reach up to the ceiling, or a cornice is present, pin scotia moulding or quadrant beading to the top edge of the battening to give a neat finish.

Punch any pinheads which show into the wood and fill with wood filler if you are varnishing the boards or an all-purpose filler if you are painting the boards.

**2** *Sand the cladding*
With all the boards and trims in place, sand the wall surface down lightly to remove the odd splinter and any marks made during installation. Use either a sanding block or an orbital sander for this. Then wipe down the board surfaces with a clean, lint-free cloth dampened with white spirit to remove dust, ready for the final finish to be applied. On horizontal or diagonal cladding, make sure you blow any sawdust out of the grooves in the cladding first.

**3** *Decorate the cladding*
All that remains is to apply the finish. If you are using paint, apply knotting, primer, undercoat and one or two top coats, rubbing down lightly between each coat.

If you are applying varnish, thin the first coat with about 10 per cent white spirit and follow this with two more full-strength coats.

If you want to stain the wood, experiment on offcuts first to get the depth of colour you want. Then apply the stain, leave to dry and sand down very lightly with very fine-grade abrasive paper if the stain has lifted the grain. Finally, varnish as before.

Complete the job by reconnecting the switch and socket faceplates removed earlier.

## BRIGHT IDEA

**Panelling round a bath** As well as wall surfaces, cladding is also perfect for panelling round a bath.
Start by constructing a simple supporting framework using 50×25mm battens fixed to the floor and side walls. Add one or two 50mm sq corner posts as required, notched to fit over the floor batten at the bottom and wedged underneath the lip of the bath at the top, and finish off by fixing top rails between the side battens and the corner post(s).
Add the cladding using the same technique as for fixing to walls, with a removable section to allow you to get to the plumbing when necessary.

# CHOOSING WOOD BY THE METRE

A guide to choosing mouldings, lippings and shaped sections of timber.

Wood mouldings are mostly sold by the metre, although many come in standard lengths. They are used as decoration or to finish off woodwork or building work. Some of the smaller mouldings, such as quadrant or scotia, are used to cover gaps or joins or to add a decorative finish to bare edges; larger mouldings, such as architrave or skirting, are used as part of the normal building of a house (but primarily to cover up a join). Other mouldings have their own specific purpose: glazing bead for holding in pieces of glass or weatherbar for throwing water off the bottom of doors.

There is a very wide range of mouldings available and only the main ones are covered here. Other more specialist mouldings are sold for cabinet making, picture framing, toy-making, stair rails and for use in sash windows and panel doors.

**Fixing** Mouldings are usually either nailed or glued in place. As they are often decorative, screws should not normally be used unless they, too, are decorative (there are dome-head screws in chrome and brass finishes, for example, or screws which have snap-on caps, available in various finishes to hide the screw head). When nailing on mouldings, usually panel pins are used (or nails with small heads). The heads should be punched below the surface and the tiny holes filled. (Blunting the sharp end of a nail by tapping gently with a hammer stops it splitting the wood – it cuts its way through rather than forcing the fibres apart.) Oval nails have the same effect.

**Type of wood** Large mouldings are usually made in softwood, small mouldings in hardwood (generally ramin or red hardwood), but sometimes these can be in softwood, too. Investigate sources of supply (timber yards and DIY stores) to see what sizes are available.

## LARGE MOULDINGS

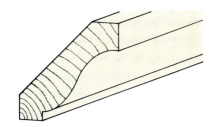

### CORNICE
**Style** A decorative softwood moulding intended to be positioned across a right angle. This is a typical example of the style of cornice most commonly used.
**In use** It is used to finish off the join between the wall and ceiling, known in the building trade as the ceiling/wall junction. Although timber cornice was used extensively in houses until the 1930s, since then it has been replaced by moulded plaster or polystyrene coving.

### SKIRTING
**Style** Available in widths 40-400mm. Styles range from the basic chamfered skirting to Victorian styles topped with decorative rounded or curved mouldings. Usually made in softwood, but some hardwood skirting is available.
**In use** For covering the junction between wall and floor and protecting the lower wall surface. Skirting can be screwed to wall plugs in a solid wall or nailed to the uprights of a hollow wall.
**Watchpoint** Some large (300mm-400mm) skirtings are made up in two or three sections, the top one of which is architrave moulding.

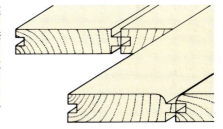

### TONGUED-AND-GROOVED
**Style** A flat softwood plank with a slot (the groove) along one edge and a matching tongue, which fits in the groove, on the other. Sizes vary from 100-150mm wide.
**In use** For floorboards (if 19mm, 22mm or 25mm thick) or for cladding walls and ceilings (if 12mm or 16mm thick). Wall and ceiling cladding is often known as matchboarding. Nails are put through the tongue of one piece and then the nail head is covered by the groove of the next – a process known as 'secret nailing'.

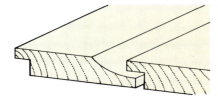

### SHIPLAP
**Style** A flat softwood plank with a rebate on one edge and a curved tongue on the other. Typical sizes are 125mm or 150mm wide and 16-25mm thick.
**In use** For cladding external walls. Unlike tongued-and-grooved, which is applied vertically, shiplap is applied horizontally. The fixing method is similar: secret nailing technique.
**Watchpoint** The boards are placed with the curved edge at the top, so that the rain runs off. Shiplap must be painted or treated with a preservative stain to protect it from the weather.

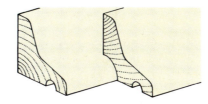

### WEATHERBAR (door drip)
**Style** A softwood moulding, typically 50×75mm with a gentle curve on the top and a groove on the bottom. Sometimes available in hardwood.
**In use** For fitting to the bottom of exterior doors to throw off the rainwater. Usually screwed in place to the door, with the counter-sunk screw holes filled with wooden plugs or stopping. When it rains heavily, water can collect on the moulding edge and then be blown by the wind under the door – the groove on the underside of the weatherbar is designed to stop this.

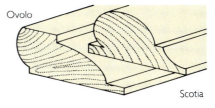

### PICTURE RAIL
**Style** A softwood moulding positioned high up on the wall. Both plain and fancy patterns are available. The two traditional, but still very popular, styles are called ovolo and scotia – the latter being the more ornate.
**In use** Designed for hanging pictures, but these days put up mainly as a decorative feature or to define the point where the decoration changes from paint to wallpaper. Usually nailed to the wall and mitred at room corners.
**Watchpoint** Needs securing well if heavy pictures are to be hung from it.

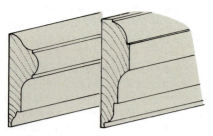
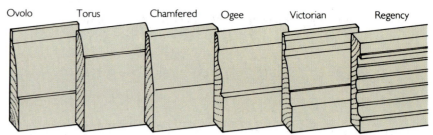

### DADO RAIL
**Style** A decorative softwood moulding, typically 63mm or 75mm wide. Also known as a chair rail.
**In use** Fixed to wall 1m above floor. Originally to protect the wall from knocks by chair backs.
**Watchpoint** Dado rails are coming back into fashion after having been removed from old houses for many years.

### ARCHITRAVE
**Style** A shaped softwood moulding, typically 50mm, 63mm and 75mm wide. Some hardwood architrave is available. Choose from the plainest chamfered sort, or Victorian, ovolo, ogee, torus and Regency styles. Ogee is used in many older houses; torus – much plainer – is more suited to modern houses.
**In use** For hiding the join between a door or window frame and the wall. It is nailed to the frame with the thick part of the moulding on the outside and is mitred at the corners.
**Watchpoint** Large and ornate architraves can usually be matched by a specialist supplier or can sometimes be bought second-hand.

## SMALL MOULDINGS

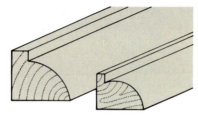
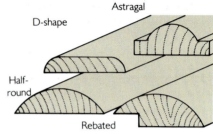

### DOWEL
**Style** A round moulding usually in hardwood. Typical sizes vary from 6-30mm wide, although larger sizes are available; some in softwood.
**In use** This has a wide range of uses; curtain poles, broom handles, plate racks and towel rails. It is also used to reinforce a glued timber joint.
**Watchpoint** Dowels for joining timber are often sold with grooves. The grooves run along the length of the dowel to allow space for excess glue to escape.

### GLAZING BEAD
**Style** A shaped softwood or hardwood moulding with a lip on one edge. Typical size 13×19mm.
**In use** For holding glass in place in windows and doors.
**Watchpoint** Thin sections can easily split unless nails are blunted. The corners should be mitred to give a neat result.

### HALF-ROUND
**Style** A softwood moulding with one flat and one curved face. The curved surface can also be D-shaped or may have a flat section either side of the curve – this is called an astragal. Sizes vary from 12-50mm wide.
**In use** For covering the edges of sheet material, such as plywood or chipboard, particularly when used for shelving, or for covering butt joints between two lengths of board. Usually glued in place, but can be nailed. Also available rebated for fitting over a panel.

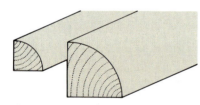
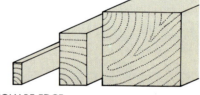
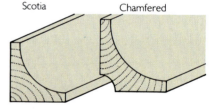

### QUADRANT
**Style** A hardwood or softwood moulding which has the cross-section of a quarter of a circle. Sizes vary from 12-50mm wide.
**In use** For covering internal corners, such as gaps between skirtings and floor boards, windows and window sills, walls and worktops or an internal joint in a timber construction.
**Watchpoint** Smaller sizes can also be used in place of glass bead.

### SQUARE-EDGE
**Style** A square or rectangular moulding in either softwood or hardwood available in a wide range of sizes, typically 25×25mm.
**In use** For finishing off shelf edges, especially those made from blockboard, chipboard, or plywood. Can also be used for glazing. Usually glued on, but may be nailed as well.
**Watchpoint** Thin rectangular hardwood mouldings are often known as lipping.

### SCOTIA
**Style** A hardwood or softwood moulding with a concave curve. Sizes vary from 13×13mm to 38×38mm.
**In use** Same uses as for quadrant, but more decorative. Can also be used as a cornice.
**Watchpoint** Some patterns have a chamfer (bevelled edge) on the right-angle corner to make them easier to fit.

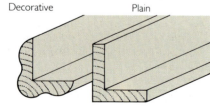
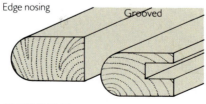
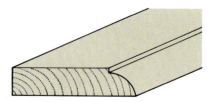

### CORNER
**Style** An L-shaped hardwood moulding, typically in sizes from 14×14mm to 35×35mm. Decorative as well as plain corner mouldings are available.
**In use** To finish off a corner where two boards join or as lipping to a work-top. (The L-shape moulding is pinned to the side and bottom edge of the exposed worktop.)

### EDGE NOSING
**Style** A softwood moulding with one curved edge and one square edge. Typical size: 32mm thick.
**In use** This is usually panel-pinned (or nailed) to the edge of shelves, particularly if they have unsightly edges. Grooved edge-nosing is used to finish off hardboard or plywood. It slots over the edges and is panel-pinned in place.

### OVOLO DOOR STOP
**Style** A decorative softwood moulding, typically 16×38mm in size.
**In use** A door stop is fitted to the inside of a door frame, where the door closes against it. Ovolo moulding provides a more decorative answer than the usual plain, rectangular moulding.

# SIMPLE CHAIR REPAIRS

Chairs and stools in everyday use often suffer from irritating faults such as loose joints or wobbly legs but these can usually be repaired quite easily.

Wooden chairs that are used in the kitchen and dining room, for example, often suffer from everyday misuse. Anything from tilting back on only two legs to dragging a chair along the floor can loosen joints and make a chair unusable. As long as the wood hasn't split, repairing joints usually only involves dismantling the chair, cleaning the joints thoroughly and gluing them together again. Depending on the joint, cramping may be necessary.

Another problem that often afflicts chairs and stools is uneven legs, making the seat wobble when you sit on it. To remedy this, you can either add a bit of wood to the leg that is short or trim a sliver off the other three.

This chapter covers repairing ordinary stick and frame chairs. If you think that your furniture may be valuable or antique, have it professionally repaired.

### WORKING WITH ADHESIVE

Most old furniture is stuck together with an animal glue, such as Scotch glue, which dries pale brown. Although still used by experienced restorers, this type of glue sets very quickly which makes it difficult for beginners to use. It is, however, easy to remove by softening with damp heat if you have to dismantle a chair to repair it.

For making new repairs to wood, a polyvinyl acetate (PVA) adhesive is the best choice for a beginner. This type of adhesive sets quite slowly which gives you time to work with more care – the adhesive sets firmly enough for a piece to be handled within a couple of hours if more work needs to be done, and sets hard within about 12 hours. On the other hand, it is difficult to remove once set (although any excess can be wiped off while still wet).

PVA adhesive is readily available from DIY shops, and comes in plastic bottles with a convenient pouring spout – it's best to buy a small bottle to avoid wastage through drying out. Although many brands are white in the bottle it dries clear.

### USING CRAMPS

Most glued joints must be cramped together, or the adhesive does not form a strong bond.

For cramping up a chair, the best tool is the sash cramp which has two adjustable metal jaws on a long bar – one jaw can be fixed in place with a pin, while the other jaw has a handle for tightening the cramp up. A couple of 900mm sash cramps are usually sufficient for most jobs, or you can buy just the sash-cramp heads (the metal jaws) and make the bars out of hardwood.

If you're not planning to do a lot of woodwork, however, you can save a lot of money by making a tourniquet-style cramp instead from rope or thick webbing and a stick.

Cramps must always be used with wood blocks, cloth pads or pieces of card to prevent the metal jaws or tourniquet from bruising the workpiece.

In addition to cramps, a portable workbench, if you have one, is useful – the long adjustable jaws which form the entire worktop can be used as a giant vice to hold components together as well as for raising the piece you're repairing to a comfortable height.

*As good as new*
*Wooden chairs that are used a lot – such as these kitchen ones – often suffer from rickety joints and legs but these faults can usually be repaired successfully and quite easily to make them as good as new.*

**CHECK YOUR NEEDS**
**For repairing loose joints:**
☐ Masking tape and felt pen
☐ Wooden mallet or heavy hammer
☐ Scrap wood or cloth
☐ Old chisel
☐ Sharp craft knife
☐ Old rags
☐ PVA woodworking adhesive
☐ Artist's paintbrush
☐ 2 sash cramps (or rope and stick for a tourniquet)

**For frame chairs** you may also need:
☐ Screwdrivers
☐ Drill and twist bits
☐ Hardwood dowelling
☐ Tenon saw

**For curing uneven legs:**
☐ Packing material (pieces of cardboard or hardboard)
☐ Pencil
☐ Tenon saw
☐ Glasspaper
☐ Offcut of wood (optional), plus fixing screw and screwdriver

## REPAIRING LOOSE JOINTS

If the joints of a chair have worked loose, it is generally best to knock the frame of the chair (or part of it) apart, clean up all the joints thoroughly and re-glue. Even if it's possible to squirt adhesive directly into a loose joint, you cannot remove the old glue, or make sure that the joint is adequately covered with new glue, without taking the chair apart.

## STICK CHAIRS

A typical stick chair is often put together entirely with dowel joints in the form of a series of spindles glued into holes drilled in the seat and top rail. The back and leg assemblies are completely independent of each other – so there's no need to remove the back spindles, for example, if only the legs are loose (or vice versa).

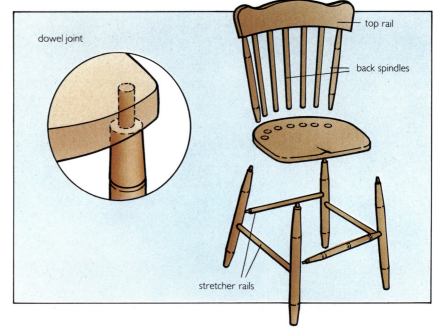

**1** *Label the parts* ▽
Before taking anything apart, it's important to identify and mark each joint so that you can reassemble the chair correctly. Spindle pieces, for example, may appear identical but they often differ slightly in size or joint detail and are particularly easy to confuse.

The simplest system for identification is to use the same letter or number for all the parts that go together to make up a joint – A-A, B-B and so on – and mark them on paper stickers or small strips of masking tape.

**2** *Dismantle the joints* ▽
You may be able to twist the spindles out of their sockets. Otherwise, hold one part of the joint and tap the other part with a mallet or hammer, using a piece of wood or a cloth folded into a thick pad to protect the piece you're striking. Don't try to lever joints apart with a chisel – this only damages the wood.

With stubborn joints, try holding the joint in the steam from a boiling kettle or placing a hot damp cloth over it for a few minutes. This should soften animal glue quite quickly – with modern adhesive, you'll have to persevere.

**3** *Clean up the joints* ▽
Having dismantled the chair, carefully clean the old glue off all the joints ready for reassembly. Scrape off any remaining large pieces of dry old glue with a knife or the tip of an old chisel, or, if you prefer, sand down with a piece of coarse glasspaper.

If necessary, put the piece in a bowl of hot water, or hold it under a running hot tap, until the glue softens enough for you to be able to wipe it away with a rag. Then allow the wood to dry out naturally and thoroughly before starting to reassemble the chair.

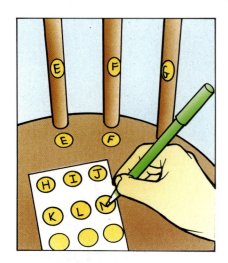

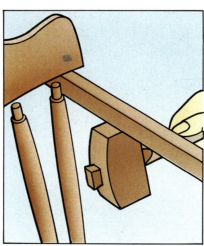

**4** *Do a test run*
Before putting the chair together again permanently, it's a good idea to reassemble it without glue to make sure that all the joints actually fit. If joints are too tight, take them apart again and lightly rub with glasspaper.

## 5 Reassemble the chair

To reassemble the chair, the back spindles can be stuck into the seat after the legs, but stretcher rails must be glued to the legs before the legs are stuck into the seat. For gluing joints and cramping, see below and Bright Idea.

Glue each stretcher rail to its legs, then glue the complete leg assembly into the bottom of the seat. Place chair upright on a flat surface to check that it's standing level: cramp stretcher rails, then weight the seat with a pile of books. Leave to dry, then glue bottom ends of back spindles and twist into seat. Glue tops of spindles, add back rail and tap into place with a mallet.

### Gluing the joints ▽

Squeeze PVA adhesive on to each part of the joint and make sure that surfaces are well covered. Push joint firmly together, or tap the glued piece into place, using a mallet or hammer with a block of wood or cloth.

If possible use a cramp (or tourniquet) while glue is drying. Leave for at least six hours to dry, and allow 24 hours before putting any load on the joint.

### Using sash cramps ▽

Although pieces can usually be tapped into place with a mallet or hammer, sash cramps are sometimes essential to hold joints steady while the glue dries.

Having glued and fitted the joints, fit sash cramps – with offcuts of wood or pieces of card under the jaws to protect the furniture – and tighten them up gradually. Make sure that the pressure is applied directly in line with the joints, or the frame will be pulled out of shape. Leave adhesive to dry for at least six hours before removing cramps.

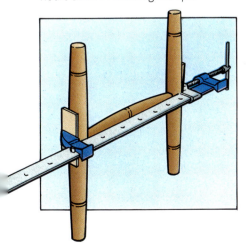

## BRIGHT IDEA

**MAKE A TOURNIQUET**
Instead of using sash cramps, make a tourniquet with a piece of rope – or use a length of upholsterer's webbing, if you have some, as this gives more even pressure over a wide area. Wind the rope or webbing around the glued parts and knot firmly, inserting a sturdy stick or small piece of dowelling into the securely tied knot.

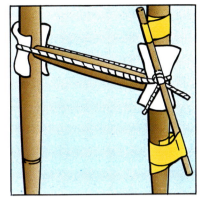

Protect the wood by placing pieces of cardboard underneath the string at corners. Then turn the stick clockwise until the string tightens sufficiently to hold the joint in place while the glue dries, and tie down or secure with a strip of masking tape to prevent the twisted string from unwinding. Be careful that you don't make the tourniquet so tight that it distorts the joint.

### FRAME CHAIRS ▽

On frame chairs, the four legs are joined together with seat rails and a drop-in seat rests on top. They generally have mortice and tenon joints (sometimes held together by pegs), and wooden corner blocks may be fitted to the inside of the seat frame to reinforce it. Before dismantling a frame chair, label all the joints as in Step 1 opposite.

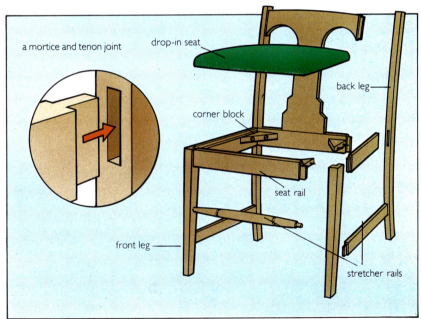

## 1 Remove corner blocks ▷

If there are wooden corner blocks or metal brackets on the inside of the seat frame, unscrew these before dismantling the chair.

They may come away as the screws are removed. If they don't, try to release the block by softening the old glue with steam from a boiling kettle or wrap a hot damp cloth round it.

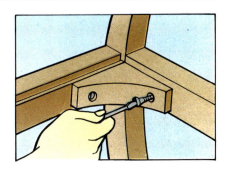

**2 Remove pegs** ▷
Check mortice and tenon joints to see whether they are reinforced with pegs – in older chairs, especially, these were sometimes put through the sides of the tenon and glued in place. If there are pegs, remove them and fit new ones later.

To remove a peg, first drill a small hole down through its centre. Then change to a larger bit – that is only just smaller than the diameter of the peg – and drill the peg out. Wrap a short piece of masking tape round the bit as a depth stop so that you don't drill right through the piece. Use a small screwdriver to clear out any bits of peg that are left behind in the hole.

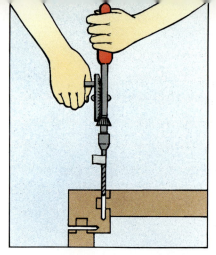

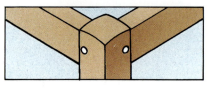

**3 Dismantle the chair**
If possible, knock apart the joints at either end of the front and back seat rails first – using a mallet or hammer with a protecting block or cloth to tap the joints apart if necessary. Then dismantle the front and back frames, and each of the side frames.

Then clean up all joints and check that they fit (see Steps 3 and 4, page 40) before reassembling with glue.

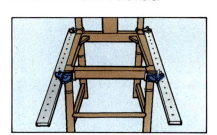

**4 Reassemble the chair** ◁
With a typical frame chair you should glue and cramp the legs and rails of each side frame, then link the two side frames together by fitting the main seat rails and any front and back stretchers and cramp up the complete assembly.

**5 Replace corner blocks**
If corner blocks have been removed earlier, refit them while the frame is in cramps. Cover the two surfaces with adhesive and press the block into position. Then drive in the screws to secure the block, taking care not to over-tighten them.

**6 Replace pegs** ▷
If pegs were drilled out to free joints, replace them with new hardwood dowels of the right diameter for the holes. Unless you're using ready-made dowels, first cut a shallow groove along the length of dowelling with a tenon saw – this allows glue to escape as dowel is pushed into hole.

Measure the depth of each hole, using a screwdriver or similar tool, and cut each dowel at least 5mm over length. Then chamfer one end at a slight angle with a sharp chisel so that the dowel will slot home without chipping. Apply glue to chamfered end, push it into hole and tap home with a hammer. Leave to dry, then trim dowel.

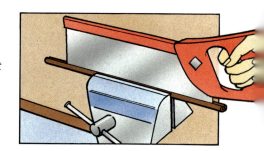

## CURING UNEVEN LEGS

If a chair or stool is wobbly because the legs have worn unevenly, the simplest solution is to cut the longer legs down to the length of the worn one.

However, this is not suitable if the chair or stool is one of a set because it would result in the repaired seat being smaller than the others. In this case, it's generally best to add a piece of wood to the short leg so that it matches the others (see Building up a short leg).

**1 Level the chair**
Stand the wobbly chair or stool on a flat surface. Use stiff card or hardboard as packing material, and insert pieces under the short leg until the chair stands steady.

**2 Mark the long legs** ▽
Take the packing material from under the short leg, and use it as a guide to mark each of the 'long' legs with a sharp pencil, moving it slowly round the base of the leg. The scribed line then remains parallel with the floor surface even if the chair legs are splayed.

**3 Cut the long legs** ▽
Use a craft knife to score a cutting line on the waste side of the pencil mark, then trim the long legs to length with a tenon saw. Complete each cut carefully to prevent splitting the wood, and sand smooth with abrasive paper. Stand the piece up to check that the wobble is cured and adjust if necessary by rubbing each leg in turn over a sheet of glasspaper laid face-up on the bench.

**4 Building up a short leg** ▽
Cut an offcut of wood to match the thickness of packing material needed to fill the gap under the short leg (see Step 1 above). Then shape it roughly to match the profile of the leg.

Sand the end of the short leg to remove dirt, then glue the offcut to it – spread adhesive on both surfaces, leave to dry, then spread on a second coat to make the join. Drill a pilot hole through the offcut into leg and drive in a screw coated with wood adhesive. When set, sand offcut to match leg profile.

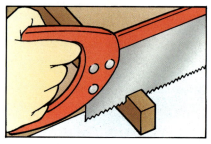

# RENOVATING OLD FURNITURE

Careful cleaning can often turn a junk shop bargain into a fine piece of furniture.

A piece of junk shop furniture may appear shabby at first sight. But very often all that is needed is careful cleaning to remove years of grime, and simple repairs to restore an attractive finish.

### ASSESS THE DAMAGE
It is important that you examine second-hand furniture carefully before you buy. Look for signs of woodworm (see below). Check stability by waggling legs and other joints, slide drawers in and out, and make sure hinges are in good order. Think twice about buying if there are deep cracks, or badly-damaged veneer or beading.

Superficial blemishes in the finish can usually be removed or disguised. But watch out for signs of more serious problems – a black or grey stain, for example, usually means that water has penetrated the wood. In these cases the furniture will have to be stripped back to bare wood and completely re-finished.

Here we cover basic cleaning and simple treatments to repair the surface of otherwise sound wood with a clear finish – such as wax polished or varnished furniture. Stripping and re-finishing old wooden furniture is dealt with in greater detail in the following chapter.

Repairs to legs, drawers, hinges and fittings must be tackled before any surface renovations.

Don't attempt to renovate furniture that might be valuable or classed as antique – these should really be restored by an expert.

**Check for woodworm** If left untreated, woodworm can easily infect other wooden structures in your home – other furniture or structural timbers – and cause serious damage. Mild cases can be treated (see overleaf), but don't take it into the house until you have done so. Never buy furniture riddled with woodworm.

Test the wood by pressing the timber around the holes – these tiny holes can conceal an inner network of tunnels and badly-infested wood will be very soft. Fine dust on the surface indicates recent activity, and the inside of a fresh hole will be light and clean. A dark hole will probably be an old one.

### IDENTIFY THE FINISH
It's important to find out what finish has been used on the furniture. Never be too hasty about removing an old finish – the deep, rich patina that builds up as wood ages cannot be instantly replaced.

There are two categories of furniture finishes: 'soft' finishes that sink into the wood (boiled and raw linseed oil, teak oil and wax), and 'hard' finishes that form a protective skin on the surface (french polish and varnish).

**Oil** allows grain and texture to show through. It has a rich glowing colour and is quite tough and water-resistant. Teak oil is a good substitute for traditional linseed oil – it dries quicker and is more resistant to marking.

*Old made new*
Don't be put off by a dull surface. This tired old chair (left) can be cleaned and polished to look good as new (right).

**Wax** has a soft, subtle sheen, and is used to protect all kinds of wood finishes. Wax is also suitable for stripped wood but, on new or raw wood, one or two sealing coats of matt polyurethane varnish before waxing provides a more durable finish.

**French polish** is traditionally used on very fine furniture and several coats provide a mirror-like surface. It is difficult to apply and is not particularly durable, being prone to scratching and marks from heat and alcohol. There are several types including button (reddish brown), garnet (dark red), white and transparent.

**Varnish** gives wood a transparent hard gloss. Old oil-varnished furniture often has a heavy brown 'sticky' appearance, or it may be covered with a cellulose varnish which is often 'crazed'. Cellulose is flammable so use french polish instead when touching up a cellulose finish.

These old varnishes have been superseded by polyurethane, available in matt, satin and gloss finish and several colours, which gives a tough durable sealing coat and is easy to apply.

**Testing the finish** Rub a small polished area which will not show, with real turpentine – if the surface has been oiled or waxed, this will take you down to bare wood.

If a polished surface still shows, test with a little methylated spirit – the surface will dissolve and go sticky if it is french polished.

Cellulose thinner will dissolve a cellulose varnish which will then usually scrape to a fine powder.

If the finish fails to respond to any of these solvents it is probably a varnish such as polyurethane.

**Safety** When using chemicals work in a well-ventilated room; make sure there are no naked flames and do not smoke. Wear rubber gloves.

*Treating woodworm* ▷

If there are signs of woodworm, treat it before you take the furniture inside the house. Squirt a proprietary woodworm-killing fluid (sold in special injector bottles) into the holes, following the manufacturer's instructions. Then brush the fluid over all unsealed surfaces.

To prevent further outbreaks, it's best to use an insecticidal polish at regular intervals.

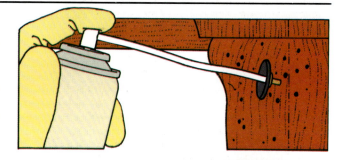

## BASIC CLEANING

Stand the furniture on newspaper or plastic sheeting. To clean off the dirt, use a mixture of four parts of white spirit to one of linseed oil. This won't lift the finish (except wax) or raise the grain of the wood.

Alternatively use a proprietary wood restorer-cleaner, following the manufacturer's instructions.

**1** *Remove surface dirt* ▷
Dust off the surface. Then rub gently with a soft cloth dampened with the oil and spirit mixture or a restorer-cleaner. An old toothbrush or a knitting needle is ideal for reaching difficult corners and mouldings.

**2** *Remove stubborn grime*
If rubbing with a cloth doesn't work, or if there is a build-up of old wax polish, use a wad of very fine 000 grade steel wool which has been moistened with the oil/spirit mixture or the restorer – cleaner.

Rub with the grain, using a light, even pressure so that you remove grease and dirt without disturbing the finish. Wipe up the excess as you work.

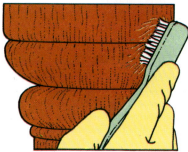

**3** *Clean up*
Wipe the surface clean with a cloth dampened with white spirit. Allow the furniture to dry naturally (with drawers removed, doors or flaps open) in a well-ventilated room.

### CHECK YOUR NEEDS
☐ Rubber gloves
☐ Newspaper or plastic sheeting
**Woodworm treatment**
☐ Woodworm-killing fluid
☐ Insecticidal polish
**Cleaning materials**
☐ White spirit and linseed oil or wood restorer–cleaner
☐ Good-sized cloths
☐ Old toothbrush/knitting needle
☐ Fine steel wool (000 grade)
☐ Wax polish
**Extras**
☐ for white marks: turpentine, white spirit and vinegar
☐ for light scratches: flour paper and linseed oil
☐ for deeper scratches and small holes: proprietary wood scratch remover or beeswax or child's wax crayon (for oiled, waxed or varnished furniture); shellac stick (for french-polished furniture)
☐ for dents: warm iron plus damp rag

## REMOVING SURFACE MARKS

These treatments are only for minor or superficial blemishes. If the surface is badly stained, or badly broken and needing a thorough repair, it should be stripped first.

### Remove white marks

White rings or patches, usually caused by wet glasses or hot cups, are often found on french-polished or cellulose finishes.

Rub marks with real turpentine and linseed oil mixed in equal parts. Clean excess off with vinegar, and repeat until the mark has gone. Proprietary ring removers are also available; use according to manufacturer's instructions.

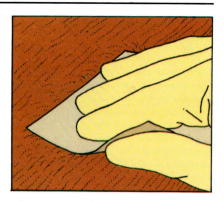

*Rub out surface scratching* △
Try rubbing out very light surface scratching using flour paper (very fine sandpaper) which has been dipped in linseed oil. Rub lightly and with the grain of the wood.

### Fill scratches and holes in wax-polished wood
Small scratches and small holes – such as woodworm holes or shallow burns – can be filled with a proprietary wood scratch remover (wax sticks in a range of wood shades), with softened beeswax or even with a child's wax crayon.

Do not use varnish on top of a wax filler – it will not stick over wax. You can, however, use wax polish over a varnished surface.

### Scratch remover ▷
Rub the wax stick well into the scratch and allow to harden. Then wipe off any surplus with a rag and buff up with wax polish.

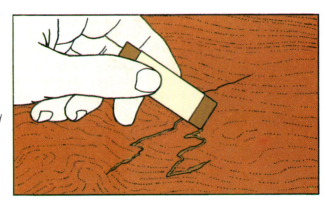

### Children's wax crayons ▷
These are very useful as they can be melted and blended together to match the colour of the wood.

Melt pieces of crayon in a heated spoon, or in a foil dish set in a pan of boiling water. When cool, mix the melted crayons together with your fingers, and apply the wax to the hole with a knife blade. Leave to set hard, then lightly smooth the surface with flour paper and re-polish with wax.

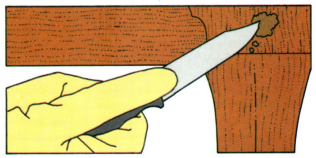

### Fill scratches and holes in french-polished or varnished wood ▷
Fill with successive layers of french polish or varnish. Modern varnish can be used directly from the tin. When using french polish, pour a little into a saucer and leave until it is semi-set (it thickens with exposure to air). On light woods use a paler shade of varnish finish as a filled scratch tends to look darker than its surroundings.

First, lightly sand the area with flour paper to smooth the edges of the scratch. Then use a small fine paint brush to drip a little polish into the scratch, and leave to dry hard before applying the next layer. Repeat until scratch or hole is filled.

To blend in the new patch with the surrounding surface, first rub it gently with flour paper that has been dipped in linseed oil and then with a soft cloth.

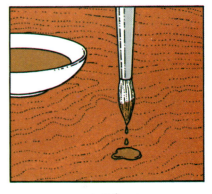

### Remove dents ▷
Dents in solid surfaces (not veneers) can usually be raised with a warm iron and a damp rag. Lay the rag over the area and press with the tip of the heated iron – this will raise the dent by forcing moisture into the wood fibres. Be careful not to scorch the surface – don't use a very hot iron or leave it there too long.

### Camouflage repairs
Coloured wax polish (or shoe polish) is useful camouflage after repairing surface blemishes. The edges of a treated area will be far less noticeable.

### Restore the shine ▷
Finally, rewax the entire surface with a coat of wax polish. Apply the polish sparingly and rub in well. Then buff to a good shine with a soft duster.

If cleaning has removed an oil or wax finish and the bare wood looks dry or faded, use a proprietary wood reviver that is designed to restore the colour to wood before this final polish with wax.

## BRIGHT IDEA

**Use shoe polish** to blend in treated marks with the surrounding surface, or to camouflage scratches on a dark surface. Use polish of a similar colour to the wood, or several toning colours for a perfect match. Rub in well, then buff up the whole surface with wax polish.

## FINAL DETAILS

Finishing touches are fun and personal and will complete the transformation of an old piece of furniture. Here are some simple ideas.

☐ For the exterior of a chest of drawers or box, for example, add some new or second-hand fittings such as ornamental brass or wooden handles.

☐ On the inside, use a spare piece of wallpaper or wrapping paper – or even special scented lining paper – as pretty and practical lining for drawers, cupboards and boxes. If the lining gets torn or dirty you can easily replace it with a new one.

☐ Wallpaper – especially if it is richly coloured, patterned or textured – shows up well on the inside surfaces of a bookcase or a glass-fronted cabinet and makes an effective backdrop to a display of china or ornaments. A remnant roll of paper is usually ample for this purpose, and can be cheaper.

☐ In hard-wear areas, such as kitchens and bathrooms, PVC self-adhesive sheeting is a good choice for covering shelves and lining drawers. To apply the sheeting, smooth paper on to the surface and press from the centre outwards with a clean cloth to remove air bubbles. Alternatively, use vinyl-faced wallpaper which doesn't have to be stuck down and can easily be changed.

☐ If wooden shelves are too badly damaged for renovation, consider re-facing them with plastic laminate. Laminates are relatively inexpensive, and available in a wide range of colours and finishes. To fix in place make sure the surface to be covered is clean, glue the laminate with a contact adhesive, and trim edges with a sharp craft knife.

**Make a template** So that you get an accurate fit with large pieces of lining paper and self-adhesive materials, cut out a brown-paper template first. Keep folding its edges until it fits exactly into angles and corners.

▽ **Background colour**
*Smart green and white-spotted lining paper in a pine dresser sets off a display of bright white china.*

## LINING A DRAWER

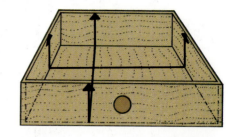

**Measure** down one side, across the base and up the other side in both directions to find the size of paper.

**Mark out** the base area of drawer, and cut diagonal slits. Fold and fit.

# STRIPPING AND REFINISHING WOOD

Old wooden furniture can be dramatically altered when stripped of layers of peeling paint or varnish.

Stripping old paint or varnish is a messy business but the end result is usually worth the time and effort. If the surface underneath is reasonably good, a clear finish can be used to enhance the colour and the grain of the wood; and even if it is to be covered up, you will still have the best possible surface for a plain or decorative paint finish.

This chapter also covers re-staining stripped wood with wood dye and/or sealing it with a clear finish – polyurethane varnish, oil or wax – to enhance and protect it.

**Stripping for action** Using a chemical solvent paint or varnish remover is the least damaging method of stripping furniture that is to have a clear finish. Blow lamps and hot air strippers are best avoided as there is a danger of scorching the surface of the wood.

You can also get furniture stripped commercially using caustic soda. This is fine for old doors and perhaps pine kitchen furniture, but too harsh for really good pieces as it can leave the wood looking slightly grey and dulled.

**After stripping** Before applying a clear finish you can alter the colour of the wood completely by bleaching it lighter or staining it darker with dye.

Any repairs, such as filling, should be made before you stain and refinish the furniture. For minor surface repairs, see Renovating Old Furniture.

### TOOLS AND EQUIPMENT

**Paint/varnish remover** to strip furniture back to bare wood: some remove both paint and varnish; others just one. Use a liquid stripper that can be washed off with white spirit. The caustic pastes that need washing down with water tend to darken the wood and are not suitable for veneers.

**Proprietary wood bleach** removes stains revealed by stripping, or lightens the wood colour so you can apply a lighter coloured stain. It usually comes as two solutions, A and B.

**Woodstopping** for filling holes and cracks is available in various wood shades. Stopping will show through a clear finish so use sparingly – a small crack or two may look better unfilled.

**Grain filler** to fill the pores on coarse-grained wood – such as oak – and provide a smooth surface for the finish; no filler is needed on close-grained wood such as pine. Available in wood shades or can be tinted to the right shade with wood dye before use.

### Natural wood surfaces

*These attractive wood pieces look best in their natural state, sealed with a clear finish, such as traditional wax polish, for protection.*

**Wood dye** can be used to tint grain filler, or to give stripped wood a richer colour while still leaving the grain clearly visible. Dyes based on white spirit are easy to use; colours range from pale pine to darkest ebony, or can be mixed to the exact shade you want. Remember dye can only be used to darken, not lighten, the wood.

**Polyurethane varnish** is a tough, durable finish, but it requires more careful application than oil or wax. Available in matt, semi-gloss and gloss finishes, it comes in clear, wood shades and various colours.

**A varnish brush** has thick bristles for smoother application, but an ordinary paint brush will do: use a 50 or 75mm brush for large areas, a 25mm one for small pieces. Keep these brushes for varnishing only.

**Oil** deepens the colour and enhances the grain of the wood. Modern oils are more durable and dry quicker than linseed oil: use danish oil for a low lustre; teak oil for a higher sheen.

**Wax** provides a soft subtle sheen. It's not a very durable finish, so is often used on wood sealed with another finish such as french polish. Available clear, or a coloured one can be used to give a dark 'antique' look to unstained wood.

### CHECK YOUR NEEDS
**For stripping:**
- ☐ Paint/varnish remover
- ☐ Old paint brush
- ☐ Paint scraper
- ☐ Steel wool, grade 3
- ☐ Nail file or toothpick
- ☐ White spirit
- ☐ 2 empty tins (eg paint tins)
- ☐ Vinyl gloves
- ☐ Plastic sheeting/newspaper

**For bleaching:**
- ☐ Proprietary wood bleach
- ☐ 2 glass jars
- ☐ Old paint brush
- ☐ White vinegar
- ☐ Bucket and sponge

**For filling:**
- ☐ Wood stopping and a filling knife (or old table knife)
- ☐ Grain filler and a coarse cloth (eg hessian)

**For staining:**
- ☐ Wood dye and a lint-free cloth (eg old cotton sheet)

**For finishing:**
- ☐ Glasspaper (medium, fine and flour paper)/sanding block
- ☐ Polyurethane varnish plus varnish brush/paint brush or wax polish plus french polish for sealing or oil
- ☐ Old cloths and rags

### USING LIQUID STRIPPER
Protect the floor by standing the piece of furniture on a sheet of plastic covered with plenty of newspaper.

**1 Remove all fittings**
Pull out drawers, unscrew hinged doors and remove metal fittings such as handles and knobs; strip separately if necessary and store in a safe place until the job is finished.

**2 Apply stripper ▷**
Pour some stripper into an old tin or glass jar. Using an old paint brush, stipple a fairly thick layer of stripper on to the surface and work it well into carvings and mouldings.

Most finishes will start to lift and bubble; some simply soften so test with a scraper after about 10 minutes. Don't leave longer – otherwise it will dry and be difficult to remove.

**3 Scrape flat surfaces ▷**
Use a paint scraper to remove the softened paint off large flat surfaces – work with the grain and take care not to scratch or gouge the wood. Put your paint scrapings in an old paint tin as you work rather than letting them drop on the floor.

Finally, dip a piece of steel wool (grade 3) in the stripper and rub along the wood grain to remove any residue paint.

**4 Clean awkward surfaces ▷**
Use grade 3 steel wool to clean up any carvings or mouldings. A small pointed tool – an old nail file or a toothpick – is handy for digging softened paint or varnish out of cracks and carvings.

**A second coat** If the old finish is very thick, several applications of stripper may be necessary. Don't try digging too hard at stubborn areas with the scraper as you can easily damage the wood which has also been softened by the liquid stripper.

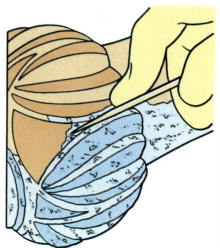

**5 Wipe down**
Following manufacturer's instructions, wipe the wood down with a rag dipped in white spirit or water to remove any trace of chemicals. Do not use water on veneers.

### SAFETY
When using stripper or bleach, wear protective vinyl gloves and old clothing. Work in a well-ventilated room (a garage is ideal), make sure there are no naked flames and don't smoke.

## BLEACHING

After stripping, use a proprietary wood bleach to remove any dark stains or to lighten the overall colour of the wood.

### 1 Apply first solution (A)
Using a 2-part bleach, decant some of the first solution (A) into a glass jar. Then apply the solution liberally to the wood with an old paint brush and leave as recommended. Rinse the brush out in water.

### 2 Apply second solution (B)
Pour the second solution (B) into another jar. Brush on to the wood, then rinse the brush out in water.

The reaction of B on A bleaches the wood. Leave until the wood is pale enough but not longer than the manufacturers recommend. If the wood is very stained or not as pale as you'd like, you can always repeat the bleaching process – re-applying both solutions, A and B.

### 3 Wash off bleach
Wash the wood down with a sponge and a solution of one teaspoon white vinegar to ½l of cold water to neutralize the bleach. Repeat using a clean sponge with a fresh solution and leave the furniture to dry thoroughly.

## FILLING THE WOOD SURFACE

If necessary, sand surfaces smooth with fine-grade glasspaper before filling. Always use a sanding block on flat surfaces and sand in the direction of the grain – never across it.

### Fill cracks and holes ▷
Press woodstopping into the crack or hole, using a knife or your finger, and scrape off any excess from the surrounding wood. When dried hard, sand it smooth with fine-grade glasspaper.

Fill deep holes in layers, allowing each layer to dry before applying the next.

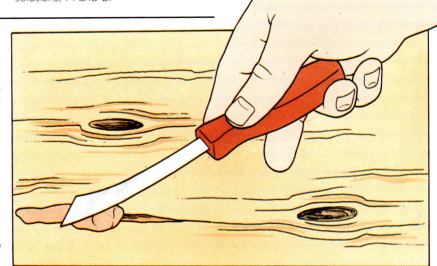

### Fill open grain ▷
Follow manufacturer's instructions for applying grain filler. Normally, you apply the filler using a coarse cloth and work over the surface with a circular polishing movement.

Remove any surplus filler with a clean cloth and allow to dry hard.

### Tinting the grain filler
Mix grain filler with wood dye before using to get a good match with more unusual wood colours. Scoop a little filler on to a clean flat surface – an old tile or pane of glass – then add stain gradually. Tint the filler slightly darker than the wood as it lightens as it dries.

Do a test so that you can check the final colour before applying to the wood: mix a small sample, leave to dry, then coat with your chosen finish.

## USING WOOD DYES

Use wood dye to colour a bleached-out stain or to give the whole piece a richer colour before sealing with the intended finish. The colour of the wood will affect that of the dye – as the dye is not removable, test an inconspicuous part of the furniture first.

### 1 Sand down
Use medium-grade glasspaper wrapped round a sanding block, and rub gently along the grain of the wood. Finish with fine-grade glasspaper in the same way, then remove all the dust with a dry paint brush.

**End grain** (a surface cut across the grain) will absorb more dye and show up darker than the rest of the wood. To avoid, seal end grain with two coats of white or transparent french polish.

### 2 Apply wood dye
Shake the dye tin well, then pour a little dye into a glass dish or a tin with a wide top. Apply the dye liberally with a lint-free cloth and rub along the grain of the wood.

When staining a large area, start at one edge and work quickly and evenly across to the other edge. Make sure that you don't go over the same area twice – overlapping will produce a dark line.

### 3 Remove surplus dye
Following manufacturer's instruction, use a clean cloth to remove surplus dye and even out the colour. Leave to dry for recommended time before sealing with your choice of finish – varnish, oil or wax.

## BRIGHT IDEA

**Age It** For a more subtle effect with dye, seal the stained wood with one coat of varnish or oil. Then add dye to some of the finish and apply to carvings and around key holes and handles with a fine artist's brush.

## A POLYURETHANE VARNISH
Seal the wood with a first coat of clear varnish thinned with 10% white spirit, before finishing with one or two full coats of clear or coloured varnish.

A varnish finish takes several days to really harden so don't put ornaments or other objects on top too soon or it will mark. Once dried hard, a thin coating of wax can be applied to mellow its appearance.

**1 Prepare the surface**
If necessary, sand all surfaces smooth with medium then fine-grade glasspaper in the direction of the grain, and round off edges. Dust off with a dry paint brush, then wipe over with a cloth dampened with white spirit. Leave to dry thoroughly.

**2 Prepare to varnish**
For best results, make sure you're working in a clean, dust-free room.

For the first sealing coat, pour some varnish into a glass jar and thin with 10% white spirit. Apply subsequent full coats straight from the tin.

**3 Apply the varnish**
Dip the brush into the varnish up to about half the length of the bristles. If the brush is overloaded, press it against the inside of the jar or tin – don't drag it across the rim as this causes bubbles in the finish.

Varnish one complete area at a time. Starting in the middle of the surface, brush along the grain towards the edges. Then brush lightly across the grain to spread varnish evenly; finish off with the grain. Avoid overbrushing.

*Wood shades* △
Wood dyes come in various standard wood colours – from palest pine to darkest ebony – but dyes of the same make can also be mixed together to get just the colour you want.

*Sand down between coats* Leave each coat to dry hard overnight, and rub very lightly with flour paper after each coat except the last. Wipe with a cloth dampened with white spirit to remove dust before applying the next coat of varnish.

*Cleaning up* Clean varnishing brushes with white spirit. Then wrap up tightly in paper so that the bristles are held in place while drying – splayed out bristles make varnishing more difficult.

---

## AN OIL FINISH
Apply two to three coats of teak or danish oil to stripped wood. Once oiled, refresh the wood with just one coat of oil when necessary or apply a thin coat of wax for a softer, more subtle sheen.

*Apply the oil*
First prepare the surface as for varnish. Then, using a clean soft cloth, apply oil liberally to the wood and rub it in well and hard along the grain. After a few minutes, wipe off excess oil with a new cloth.

Leave for 4 to 8 hours until the oil has completely dried. Then apply two or more coats of oil to build up a good hard coating – allow each coat to dry thoroughly before applying the next one.

## A WAX FINISH
For a more durable finish, first apply a sealing coat of white or transparent french polish with a soft cloth. Then finish with wax. To keep a wax finish looking good, apply a very fine coating of wax every couple of months.

*Apply the wax*
Prepare the wood surface as for varnish, and make sure that the wood is completely dry before waxing.

Then spread wax polish sparingly on to the wood with a cloth – or use an old toothbrush where there are carvings and mouldings. Polish with a soft cloth, working the wax well in, and leave for a few days to harden before applying a second coat in the same way. Finally, buff up well with a duster for a good shine.

# BAMBOOING AND VINEGAR GRAINING

Turn second-hand furniture into original, customized pieces with one of these unusual paint techniques.

These two paint techniques are best suited to furniture. Each was developed in response to a particular demand – first bambooing, in the 18th century, as a result of interest in chinoiserie among royalty and the upper classes. Vinegar graining was developed in the 19th century in response to a demand for wood effects among the middle classes – it was a much faster technique than woodgraining using traditional glazes. Bambooing is a fine technique, suited to delicate pieces of furniture, while vinegar graining is much more robust and is generally used on chunky furniture.

## BAMBOOING

This may be a trompe l'oeil effect, using realistic tones to imitate bamboo, or a fantasy effect, using artificial colours. The bands and knots of natural bamboo are reproduced, usually in unrealistic colours (blue on a white background or pink and pale green, for example). It can only be used on light pieces of furniture such as chairs and tables. The best fantasy effects are achieved on pieces of furniture made from natural bamboo – plant stands or cabinets with panels of rattan, for example. During the height of its popularity, the technique was applied to furnishings and fittings carved or cast to look like bamboo: the staircase of Brighton's world-famous Pavilion, built in the early 19th century, is a renowned example.

Bambooing is a fine technique, which takes care to perfect, so it is not a good idea to start without practising on a small piece first.

The surface to be painted has to be thoroughly prepared first: rub down with fine glasspaper to get a smooth base on which to paint. Rub down real bamboo with methylated spirit and wire wool. Prime any bare wood (any knots should first be given a coat of knotting). Undercoat and base coat are then applied – and oil-based, eggshell finish in a pale shade is best for the base coat. Build up at least three layers of paint, rubbing down with wet-and-dry paper between each coat. Ensure the surface is completely free of dust and grease before starting to paint.

The actual detail of the bamboo can be added in various ways. The effect to aim for is bands of graduated colour at each of the ring-joints of the bamboo (you will have to decide where to position these if you are not using natural bamboo or bamboo-turned wood). Running down the length of the bamboo, you paint tapering V-shapes from the ring-joints, to represent the spines of the bamboo, while small knots or eyes are dotted randomly over the surface of the wood, fairly close to the spines.

Traditionally, oil-based glaze was used, mixed with eggshell paint to give a certain opacity, and tinted with artists' oil paints or universal stainers. More paint was added to create progressively darker and more opaque mixtures for the different elements of the bamboo details. However, it is not essential to use the traditional glaze for this effect: artists' oils mixed with varnish produce a similar result, and you can also use artists' acrylic paints, thinned with water. The latter have the advantage of being quick-drying, so you can paint the different shades in a matter of hours. Whatever technique you use (and in this chapter the technique for acrylic paints is described) you then have to give the item two or three coats of silk or gloss polyurethane varnish to protect the paintwork from accidental damage and wear and tear.

*Regency style*
*In the Brighton Pavilion, the Prince Regent surrounded himself with chinoiserie: this staircase is actually made of cast iron, painted using traditional materials and techniques to imitate real bamboo.*

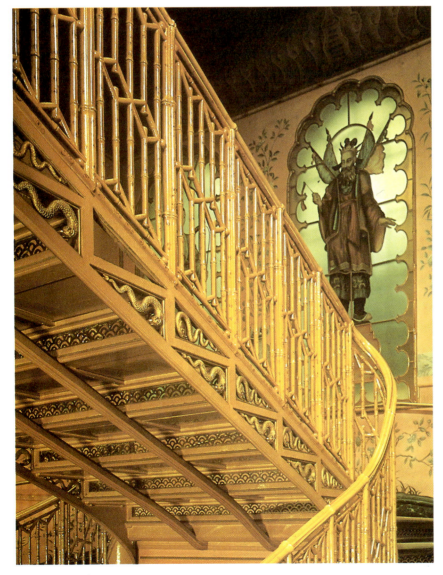

## VINEGAR GRAINING

The technique of vinegar graining was developed by furniture makers in the 19th century looking for a quick and easy way to meet a demand for 'grained' woodwork and furniture. It was particularly popular in America. It is a technique best applied over a limited area in any one room, on fairly solid pieces of furniture and fittings, such as chests of drawers, blanket chests, wardrobes or traditional, built-in alcove cupboards.

On larger pieces of furniture, you can get a more interesting effect if you vary the pattern on different parts of the structure. Use bolder patterns on flat, panelled sections and more restrained graining on the framework and moulding, for example.

The colour (in the form of powder paint) is mixed with ordinary vinegar (or beer), rather than the traditional, slow-drying glaze normally used for wood-graining. A little sugar and a dash of washing-up liquid are added to help the glaze adhere to the surface. If you are using beer rather than vinegar, opt for brown ale, since it has a greater sugar content, and you will not need to add extra sugar.

This 'glaze' is then washed over the surface of the item, and a pattern is stamped or rolled on to the wet surface. It is worth experimenting with different materials to see which makes the most attractive pattern: the most traditional materials are putty and rags, but you can use modelling clay or a scrunched-up plastic bag – in fact, almost anything that adds texture to the surface of the paint.

The technique hardly tries to imitate the natural figuring in real wood. It is instead a robust and amusing parody of graining which is within the capabilities of almost anyone. It is also very quick to apply, and of course if you are not happy with the effect you can easily paint over it and start all over again.

As with all paint techniques, the surface to be decorated must be well prepared first. Rub down with fine glasspaper, knot and prime any bare wood, and then apply undercoat. The base coat on which you paint should be a flat, oil-based paint. Use oil-based eggshell paint, and then cut through the shine by rubbing it smooth with soapy water and wet-and-dry paper. The less sheen the surface has, the better the vinegar glaze will adhere.

Before tackling a piece of furniture, it is advisable to try the technique on a sample board. You can experiment with the proportions of the glaze and check on the drying time.

More important, though, sample boards give you the opportunity to test different ways of making patterns in the glaze. Common techniques include making a sausage of putty or Plasticine and rolling it over the wet surface for a rope effect; stamping a blob of putty over the surface, either regularly or at random; patting the surface with crushed or folded paper, or a screwed up polythene bag; or combing the paint with a cardboard comb for a dragged effect. You can improvise with anything that comes to hand: pieces of string, feathers, or even your fingers. Bunch your fingers tightly together and use just your fingertips in some areas, and soften the effect by dabbing the surface with the fleshy pads of your fingers in other areas.

As with bambooing, the painted item must be varnished to protect the finish. In fact, vinegar graining will simply rub off if it is not protected. Use gloss or silk-finish polyurethane varnish. Three coats are the minimum for vinegar-grained furniture: apply two extra coats on pieces which are likely to be subjected to heavy wear.

## A SENSE OF COLOUR

The colours you choose for either of these techniques depend on the overall effect you are after and the decor of the room it has to fit into – you want the painted items to blend with other furnishings, rather than stand out.

**Bamboo tones** For a natural bamboo effect choose pale yellow ochre for the base coat, adding rings and knots in tones of amber and umber. You will have a much wider range of tones to choose from if you use and mix artists' colours (either oils or acrylic).

Particularly popular tones for a more fantastic effect are white for the base coat, with tones of grey, pink or blue for the rings and eyes. For a more opulent effect, in imitation of some of the Far Eastern styles, you could paint the bamboo black or lacquer red with gold details, or in tones of turquoise or jade with contrasting details. Finish the work with high gloss polyurethane varnish if you choose one of these more exotic colours.

**Colours for graining** Because of the rather crude method and rough shapes produced by this method, vinegar graining looks best if the tones are kept fairly subtle: dark blue, say, over a paler tone of the same colour, or a medium tone over a white base are particularly effective. And of course you can imitate the tones of natural wood, using ochres and umbers. But the general principle is to apply darker colours, lifting them to reveal the paler tones which lie beneath.

### CHECK YOUR NEEDS
- Dust sheets/newspaper
- Lint-free rags
- Rubber gloves
- White spirit

**Preparation for either effect:**
- Fine glasspaper
- Knotting and primer (if painting bare wood)

**For finishing either effect:**
- Silk-finish or gloss polyurethane varnish
- Clean (preferably new) brush for varnishing
- Glasspaper
- Tack rag (soaked in white spirit)

**For bambooing:**
**Preparation and base coat:**
- Wire wool and methylated spirit (for natural bamboo)
- Undercoat and oil-based eggshell paint for base coat
- 2cm paint brush
- Wet-and-dry paper and soapy water

**Decoration and finish:**
- Acrylic paints, ready to mix up three different tones
- 1cm paint brush
- Two artists' brushes, no3 and no6

**For vinegar graining:**
**Base coat:**
- Undercoat and oil-based eggshell paint in pale colour
- 5cm and 2cm decorators' brushes
- White spirit
- Wet-and-dry paper and soapy water
- Vinegar

**For the glaze and decoration:**
- Vinegar
- Sugar and washing-up liquid
- Powder paint
- Two bowls or jam jars for mixing the glaze
- Old spoon for mixing
- Scrap paper for testing glaze
- Clean decorators' brushes
- Pieces of putty, Plasticine etc for making patterns.

## FANTASY BAMBOO EFFECT

This effect is made easier to achieve by the use of quick-drying artists' acrylic colours.

### 1 Prepare the piece
Rub down previously painted items with fine glasspaper. Strip polished finishes, particularly wax polish, as this prevents the paint from taking. Apply knotting and prime if necessary.

### 2 Preparing natural bamboo ▷
If you are painting bamboo which has not been painted before but has been polished, rub it down with fine wire wool dipped in a little methylated spirit to get it completely clean and ready to take a coat of paint. Prime the surface, or use a dual purpose primer/undercoat.

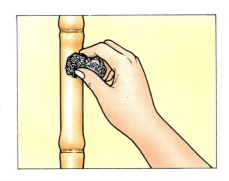

### 3 Build up the base coat
The base coat should normally be a pale tone (in this case white). It must have a matt finish, and be oil-based for durability. You can simply use undercoat for the base coat, or finish the undercoat with an oil-based eggshell paint. Whatever you choose, it is important to build up at least three layers of paint, and you must rub down well between coats: for a fine, smooth finish, rub down with wet-and-dry paper dipped in soapy water. If you choose eggshell as the top coat, rub this down lightly to reduce the sheen. After applying the base coat, wipe down thoroughly to ensure the item is free of dust and grease. Then decide on the positions for the rings (on wood): they are usually about 15cm apart, and may be evenly or unevenly spaced.

### 4 Paint the first bands △
If you are not using natural bamboo, mark the centre of each ring in pencil. Then start to paint, using a pale acrylic paint (in this case blue). Use a brush about 1cm wide to paint a fairly broad ring (about 2.5cm wide) round the bamboo beside each ring. Repeat round all the rings on the piece, and allow to dry.

### 5 Add darker bands △
Using a slightly darker and less translucent mixture, add a narrower band overlapping the pale bands already painted, so that the paler bands appear to get gradually darker towards the actual ring mark. Repeat for each band, and allow to dry.

### 6 Pick out the rings and spines △
Use the darkest tone and a fine artists' brush, with a minimum of water, to pick out the notch line round the ring of bamboo. At the same time, using the same tone, pick out very fine, V-shaped spines running along the length of the bamboo, from the rings (see step 7). One or two spines from each ring should be adequate.

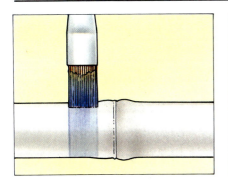

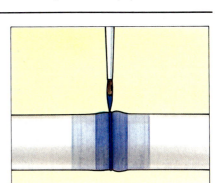

### 7 Paint in the eyes △
The 'eyes' are usually represented by a blob of pale or mid-tone paint, with a dot in the centre and two or three dots around the eye in the darkest tone. One or two eyes, fairly close to each spine, are plenty. Plan the positions carefully before you apply the paint.

### 8 Apply protective varnish △
When you are happy with the effect and the paint is completely dry, apply at least three coats of protective varnish, rubbing down lightly with glasspaper between coats. Use silk or gloss-finish polyurethane varnish. (Low sheen is better for paler tones, but if you have been bold enough to use oriental blacks, jades and golds, use gloss varnish for a lacquered effect.)

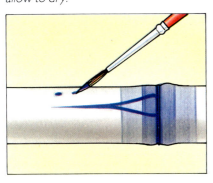

## BRIGHT IDEA

### FAKE THE SHAPE
If you're painting plain pieces of wood or inexpensive furniture with a fake bamboo finish, you can add to the illusion by shaping the wood slightly to imitate the bamboo further. You need to be patient, and fairly clever with your hands. Mix some plaster of paris to a fairly liquid consistency, and use your finger to apply a little to the wood at the point where you want the joint to be. It dries quickly, so you can build up several layers. Then carve the plaster with a sharp craft knife, and rub down with fine glasspaper. Prime the plaster and wood, then paint the rings as for real bamboo.

**VINEGAR GRAINING**
Try out the technique and decide exactly how you are going to apply the pattern before you start to work on a piece of furniture.

**1** *Prepare the surface*
Rub down the surface thoroughly – have pieces of furniture stripped professionally in a caustic tank if there is a build-up of layers of paint. It is important to start with a dust- and grease-free surface. Apply knotting if necessary, and prime any bare wood. Apply undercoat and finish with a flat, oil-based paint: this could be undercoat, or an oil-based eggshell paint, rubbed down with wet-and-dry paper and soapy water to reduce the sheen. When dry, wipe with vinegar.

**2** *Mix the glaze* ▷
In a small bowl or jam jar, mix together 100ml vinegar, 5ml sugar and a squeeze of washing-up liquid. Put a couple of teaspoons of powder colour in another bowl and slowly stir in the vinegar mixture to make a thin glaze, mixing thoroughly so there are no lumps, until you think the consistency is about right – it should be something like single cream.

**3** *Test the glaze*
Brush the glaze on to a sheet of scrap paper, brushing it out quite thinly. Pick up the sheet and hold it vertically. If the colour runs it is too thick and you will need to thin it with more vinegar.

**4** *Apply the glaze* ▽
Use a clean, 2cm-wide paint brush to apply the glaze thinly and evenly over the surface. Leave for a couple of minutes to become tacky. Do not worry if brush strokes show at this stage – this will only add to the finished, broken effect.

**5** *Add the pattern* ▽
Using putty, your fingers or whatever you find works well, start to roll or print the pattern on the fresh paint. If you aren't happy with the effect, wipe off the paint and start again, or apply more vinegar glaze. Also apply more glaze if it dries too quickly.

**6** *Allow to dry*
When you are happy with the effect, leave the item to dry out thoroughly: this should take about an hour. The colours will deaden as they dry.

**7** *Protect the finish*
To protect the finish, apply at least three coats of silk-finish polyurethane varnish, rubbing down lightly between coats. The varnish will bring life back to the colours of the graining.

▽ *With the grain*
This built-in radiator shelf and the ornate grating in front of it have been 'grained' in a random style, imitating the grain of the picture frame. Satin-finish polyurethane varnish protects the paint.

# WOOD FINISHES: TRADITIONAL LOOKS

Both new wood and renovated furniture take on extra warmth when properly stained and polished.

New wood looks almost unnaturally clean, while old wooden furniture often has to be so heavily treated to remove unwanted finishes that it, too, can look sparkling. However, part of the charm of wood is the rich colouring which comes with years of careful polishing. The depth of colour enhances the grain, and the patina which builds up over the years is quite different from the brash glossiness of modern polyurethane varnish. To re-create a traditional look (or give an antique look to new furniture) the wood has to be stained before the final finish is applied.

## KNOW YOUR WOOD

It is useful, when working with wood, to have some idea of the texture and quality of the wood obtained from different types of tree.

**Softwood** Most of the wood available from your local timber merchant is likely to be softwood, particularly pine or deal. Softwoods come from coniferous trees, which have a particularly fast growth period during the spring. This gives the tree wide rings, and wide bands of marking on the wood cut from it – paler wood for the spring growth, getting gradually darker. If you are buying softwood, avoid pieces with large knots: the knots will darken with age and may even fall out. Furthermore, because the grain in knots runs in a different direction to the grain in the surrounding wood, you will have difficulty both working and finishing the surface. Although they are called softwoods, some are quite hard (and some hardwoods are very soft).

Many ordinary pieces of Victorian furniture were made of pine which was then painted. During the 1970s the fashion was to strip away the layers of paint and polish the furniture with a beeswax polish. Now, however, the trend is again towards the painted finish which was originally intended.

**Hardwood** At your local timber merchant, the most frequent use of hardwood (often ramin) is for fine mouldings and beadings, which are difficult to produce from pine because of its knots and open grain. For new hardwood you will have to go to a specialist timber merchant. However, you may have renovated a piece of furniture made of hardwood, or you may want to polish shelves which have a hardwood finish, such as teak-veneered chipboard.

Hardwoods most commonly used for old furniture include oak, mahogany, ash, elm and beech. There are also more ornate woods, such as maple, walnut, cherry and rosewood, which have always been kept for better pieces because they are more expensive woods.

## CHOOSING STAINS

Professional woodworkers have developed their own recipes for staining wood, but there are also many proprietary brands available at good DIY stores. The type of stain you choose depends on the type of wood you are staining and the effect you are after, as well as cost and ease of use of the stain. Most dyes come in rectangular screw-top tins, and you should always follow the manufacturer's instructions.

**Water-based stains** are available ready-mixed, although some professionals prefer to use powders that they mix themselves. They are reasonably priced

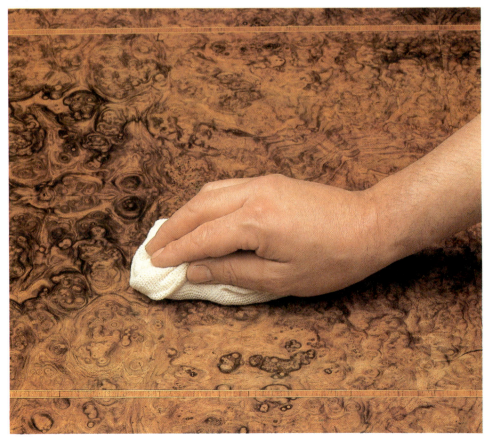

*Warmth of wood*
*The intricate pattern of highly figured walnut veneer needs careful treatment to show it off. Remove old finishes very carefully before re-finishing with french polish, wax or (in this case) oil.*

and penetrate the wood well. Water-based stains go a long way in terms of the area covered by 500cl, and they can be mixed together to create a wide range of colours.

However, because of the water content, they tend to raise the grain of the wood when applied, which means that the stain is taken up unevenly. The best solution to this is to dampen the surface to be stained first, then rub down very well with glasspaper so that when you do apply the stain, there is less chance of the grain rising.

**Oil-based stains** These have the advantage that they don't raise the grain, but on the other hand the colour does not penetrate so deeply into the wood. They are not suitable if you want to apply a wax polish, as the wax may draw out the stain.

**Spirit stains** dry quickly and they do not raise the grain. They can be used on a surface which is slightly greasy or waxy. However, because they dry quickly it is difficult to keep a 'wet edge' going, and you may find that you get a blotchy finish if you do not work confidently. They also fade more than water- or oil-based stains.

When staining wood, the closer the grain, the more evenly the wood will take up the stain. Open-grained pine, for example, will take up more stain in the soft, pale (spring growth) areas than in the closer grain. With highly figured wood it is advisable to use a stain which is less penetrating (such as an oil-based stain).

## FINAL FINISH

After staining (or indeed without staining), there is a wide choice of finishes you can apply. Here we look at preparing the surface for the final finish and the techniques involved in one traditional finish: french polish.

Alternatives to french polishing, such as oiled and waxed finishes as well as coloured and plain polyurethane varnishes for wood are discussed earlier, see Stripping and Refinishing Wood, page 50.

### CHECK YOUR NEEDS
☐ Furniture stripped of previous finish (or new wood to be treated)

**For preparation:**
☐ Wire wool
☐ White spirit
☐ Sanding block and fine glasspaper
☐ Power sander or attachment for electric drill (optional)
☐ Grain filler and canvas cloth

**For staining:**
☐ Water- or oil-based stain
☐ Cloths for cleaning and polishing
☐ Cloth or brush to apply stain

**For french polishing:**
☐ French polish
☐ Cotton wool
☐ Cotton cloth or handkerchief
☐ Linseed oil
☐ Methylated spirit

## PREPARATION

Whatever finish you intend to apply, careful preparation is essential. On old furniture, any existing finish should be removed first: use one of the heavy-duty paint removers for painted furniture, or a specialist paint and varnish remover which removes all finishes (paint, polyurethane, cellulose varnish, french polish, etc).

**1 Cleaning with wire wool** ▷
After you have stripped the existing finish (as described on page 48), rub the surface down with fine grade wire wool dipped in white spirit: this removes any stripper which is left on the surface without raising the grain. Work with the grain.

**2 Using a sanding block**
For a good finish, on both renovated and new surfaces, a thorough sanding is essential. For hand sanding, use progressively finer grades of glasspaper, wrapped around a sanding block.

If you do not want to buy a special sanding block, you can easily improvise with a block of cork, or an offcut of wood with a piece of foam or fabric wrapped around it to make a block with a bit of 'give'.

Always rub in the direction of the grain.

**3 Using a power sander** ▷
On flat, new, wooden surfaces and furniture which is not valuable, you can use an orbital sander (right, top). This has a rectangular sanding surface which moves in an orbital motion. Replace the sheets of glasspaper as they get clogged; start with a medium grade and progress to finer grades.

For very heavy work, professionals generally use a belt sander (right, bottom), which has a removable belt of glasspaper which runs over rollers at each end of the sander.

Always work with the grain.

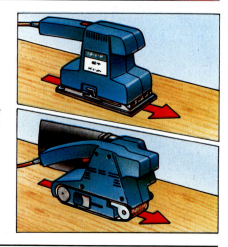

**4 Using a disc sander** ◁
If you do not have (and do not want to buy or hire) any specialist power tools, you can get a sanding attachment to use with a power drill. Avoid using disc sanders on large, flat areas such as doors or table tops, as it is difficult to get an even finish – swirls tend to appear where the edge of the disc bites into the surface.

If you do use a disc sander, hold it at a slight angle, so that only part of the abrasive disc somes into contact with the wood. Apply a minimum of pressure and keep the machine moving with the direction of the grain, so that it does not create marks in the wood.

**5** *Drum attachment for drill* ▷
You can also get drill-mounted drums, which have the advantage of sanding only in one direction. They are useful for curved surfaces, such as banisters or chair backs.

**6** *Grain filling*
If you want a smooth finish, and the wood has natural lumps and unevenness along the grain, you can use a grain filler before staining and applying other finishes. Grain filler is a proprietary paste, which is thinned with white spirit and then rubbed into the surface with a canvas cloth. Choose between natural, mahogany, oak and teak shades.

**7** *Clear the surface*
When the grain filler has gone dull, rub off the surplus with a clean canvas cloth, working across the grain. The surface, whether it is new or old wood, is now ready for a new finish. Note that if you intend to use wax polish on the surface, you do not need to fill the grain, as the polish will do this over the years.

## USING PROPRIETARY STAINS

Always test proprietary stains first on offcuts of similar wood, to check that you will achieve the right effect before you start work. You should also test the effect of the final finish you intend to apply over the stain: most finishes tend to darken stained – or unstained – surfaces. Here we give instructions for water- and oil-based stains – spirit stains are less popular and are consequently not so readily available.

**1** *Choose the colour*
Decide on the colour you want the finished article to be: most commonly, you are likely to be staining new or freshly stripped pine, to give it a mellow finish. For pine, avoid red tones of stain, such as mahogany, which are better for close-grained woods. Several manufacturers produce 'antique' pine tones – but you may find these are not quite what you had in mind. Test them, and, if necessary, mix different tones until you get the right effect.

**2** *Raise the grain*
If you are using a water-based stain, it is a good idea to raise the grain and sand before staining. Wipe the surface with a damp cloth so that a little water soaks into the wood. Allow to dry thoroughly, then sand the surface by hand.

**3** *Apply the stain* ▷
Whatever type of stain you are using, start with a clean, dust- and grease-free surface. Pour some stain into a saucer or small dish and apply it with a brush or a cloth. Work with the grain, and work quickly so that the stain does not dry out before you have started on the adjacent area. (If it does, you will get a blotchy line where you have applied two coats of stain.)

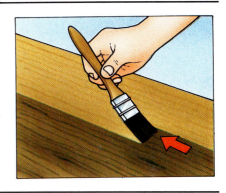

**4** *Remove excess stain*
With a water-based stain, wipe off the excess stain at once by rubbing a clean, dry rag over the surface.

**5** *Leave to dry*
Leave the stained surface to dry (a couple of hours for a water-based stain, at least six hours for an oil-based stain).

Then check the effect and apply a further coat to darken the colour if necessary, until you have the shade you want.

## FRENCH POLISHING

French polishing is normally used to give a high gloss finish to fine (hardwood) furniture: it's not a finish you would want to apply to a modern pine dresser, for example, or a renovated pine chest. It was introduced in the early 19th century, and gives a very attractive finish, showing off the grain of the wood well, but it is not resistant to either heat or alcohol. The polish used for french polishing is made from shellac, which is derived from lac insects in the East. Several thin coats of the polish are applied with a pad of material. It takes a certain amount of practice to get a perfect finish, so try out the technique first on a small, less valuable piece of furniture, before starting on the family heirlooms!

When applying french polish it is important to work in a clean, dust-free environment. It should also be a warm, dry room, as coldness will stop the polish 'flowing' and dampness will make it go cloudy when it is applied.

**1** *Make a rubber* ▷
Take a handful of ordinary cotton wool, and place it in the middle of a square of clean, fluff-free cotton cloth – a gent's handkerchief is ideal. Fold the edges of the cloth over the cotton wool and roll them together: this side goes in the palm of the hand, giving a smooth surface on the other side – the sole of the 'rubber'.

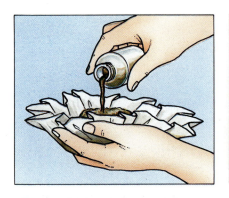 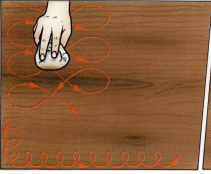 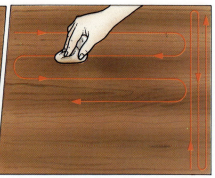

**2 Charge the rubber** △
Open out the rubber, and pour french polish on to the cotton wool so that it is fairly well soaked. Then wrap the cloth round the cotton wool again. When you squeeze the rubber slightly the polish should ooze out through the cloth. Lubricate the rubber by dipping your finger in linseed oil, and dabbing it on to the sole of the rubber.

**3 Apply the polish** △
The polish will set into ridges if it is allowed to flow too freely on to the surface of the furniture: it is important to keep the rubber moving at all times, working in oval and figure of eight movements, and gliding the rubber on and off the surface so there is no hard edge.
You will find that the polish flows freely through the rubber at first but as you continue, you will have to apply more pressure to the cotton wool inside the rubber to make the polish flow out.
Once the surface is thinly coated, finish the ends working across the grain (far right) and then work in long even strokes with the grain. When you have covered the surface, leave it to dry.

**4 Build up further coats**
The polish will take about 20 minutes to dry. When it is dry, apply a further coat in the same way. Apply up to five coats in one day, then leave to harden overnight before repeating the process: you should build up about 15 coats altogether.

**5 Finish with methylated spirit**
The next stage is known as 'spiriting off'. When you are happy with the polish, apply a few drops of methylated spirit to the rubber. Polish up and down the grain with long, even strokes. The methylated spirit dissolves the polish slightly, so the rubber should slide easily over the surface. Never let it rest in one place, or it will take off too much polish. If it starts to drag, apply more methylated spirit. This process removes the linseed oil from the surface. Finally, rub up the surface with a soft duster, then leave to harden for a week.

## BRIGHT IDEA

**LIMING WOOD**
Liming is a traditional finish for wood which lightens the tones rather than darkening them as stain does. It is traditionally applied to oak and is really a specialized method of grain filling. Work outside to prevent the lime splashing surfaces and to allow any fumes to disperse.
First bring out the grain by wetting the wood. Brushing it with a wire brush first will open the grain even further. Then mix ordinary garden lime with water to make a creamy solution which you can paint on to the surface. Leave it to dry, then rub down lightly so that you clean the lime off the surface where the grain has been raised. Finish with thinned white shellac; polyurethane yellows the wood.

▷ **Shining example**
An elegant, highly polished occasional table adds a welcoming touch to a hallway. French polished surfaces must be carefully looked after, as heat, water and alcohol will all mar the finish.

# RENOVATING IRON AND STEEL

These metals are very durable, but without proper care they can deteriorate badly.

Iron and steel are used much more widely in the average home than you might at first think, for they feature both in its construction and furnishing, with polished, painted, or lacquered finishes.

### IRON IN THE HOME
Iron and steel crop up in many places. Some houses have metal window frames; others may have cast-iron fireplaces inside, gutters and downpipes and perhaps railings outside, and wrought-iron gates. Modern central heating systems feature mild steel radiators; old ones have steel pipes and cast-iron radiators.

These metals are not widely used for furniture nowadays, but they still crop up: old iron bedsteads, modern tubular steel beds, high-tech storage systems, chairs and light fittings.

In the kitchen metal is the most common material used for cooking utensils. There are likely to be tin-plated mild steel baking pans, frying pans and woks; and cast-iron casseroles. The sharpest knives are made of carbon steel.

Mild steel is the basic metal used to make nails and screws, brackets, hooks and other fittings, utility door and window furniture and the cabinets of white goods like cookers and fridges.

### KNOW YOUR METALS
**Iron** Iron is a pure metal. Cast iron is iron mixed with a small amount of carbon and traces of other metals. It is hard and heavy, but brittle, and breaks if dropped on a hard surface. Wrought iron is iron mixed with silicate slag. It is very malleable and so used for decorative but durable items like gates. Galvanized iron has a coating of zinc to prevent rust.
**Steel** Mild steel (also known as carbon steel) is iron mixed with a minute percentage of carbon which makes it easier to work. This is the basic all-purpose utility metal formed into bars, rods and sheets.

The simplest way of recognizing iron and steel is that if unprotected by a decorative finish or by oil and grease, they develop rust spots almost immediately when exposed to water or damp air. Slight surface rust can be removed fairly easily with abrasive paper, but if left untouched it eats into the metal.

### CHOOSING A FINISH
Because iron and steel rust so easily, it is essential to give them a moistureproof coating after renovation. You can either keep the look of the metal, with oil, blacklead, or varnish, or use a proprietary paint finish, specifically designed for metal. You can also prime the metal using a metal primer and then undercoat and top coat the metal with ordinary household gloss or satin finish paints – to match the woodwork in the room, for example.

### TOOLS AND EQUIPMENT
There are no specialized tools needed for renovating iron and steel, but you will need plenty of rags, old brushes (including toothbrushes) and a wire brush and some wire wool. Many of the materials (paints, rust treatments and so on) are more expensive than the equivalent materials for treating wood, so limit yourself to small items to start with.

### CHOOSING A TREATMENT
There are various different treatments you can give iron and steel fixtures and furniture, depending on the condition of the item and the type of finish you want. Paint can be rubbed down or completely stripped off if it is in bad condition or if you want a metallic finish. Most important, however, is to get rid of any rust; this can be done in a number of ways, depending on the extent of the rust and the shape of the item being treated.

*Irons for the fire*
*A well-polished cast-iron fireplace is a welcoming sight. To keep the shine; polish the metal with black lead, or varnish it for added protection. The wooden surround is a pleasant contrast to the look of the metal – and a touch of brass adds a fiery glow, even when the fire is not lit.*

**CHECK YOUR NEEDS**
For removing paint from iron:
☐ Chemical stripper and brush
☐ Metal dish to soak small items
☐ Old toothbrush
☐ Dry rags
☐ Hair dryer (optional) OR
☐ Blowtorch or hot air blower
☐ Paint scraper
☐ Hardboard to protect fitted carpets, if necessary

For tackling rust:
☐ Wire brush, steel wool and/or emery paper OR
☐ Patent rust remover and cloths OR
☐ Special rust-proof paint, brushes and cleaner.

For finishing iron:
☐ Appropriate finish, plus brush or cloth (see section on finishes)
☐ Appropriate brush cleaner

## STRIPPING PAINT FROM IRON WORK

Stripping paint from metal is usually easier than from wood because there is no grain for the paint to sink into and get a tenacious grip. It can still be quite time-consuming if there are multiple layers to get through, but it is well worth doing with decorative items because only stripping will reveal the original outlines long obscured by paint. There are several different techniques and you may find you need to use a combination of the following methods.

**1 Using chemical strippers** ▽
Conventional semi-liquid paint strippers work well on metal, particularly small items like over-painted door furniture which can be soaked in a bath of the stuff. (Do not use a plastic container – it will quickly dissolve! Old baking tins or foil pie dishes are ideal.) Use as directed. An old toothbrush is good for working paint out of crevices, even though the stripper will eventually attack the plastic and cause the bristles to drop out. If the product is washed off with water make sure to dry it quickly and thoroughly, otherwise rust will get a hold. (A hair dryer is useful for large items; stand small ones over radiators or put them in a cool oven.)

Unfortunately the new paste strippers, which are so good at removing multiple layers of paint in one go, are not recommended for metal as they turn it black. But if discoloration does not matter – say on an old cast-iron fireplace – go ahead.

**2 Abrasion** ▽
Removing paint with abrasive paper, even in a power tool, is the least effective method of completely stripping an item. But if the paint is flaking badly and not too thick, scraping off the worst and finishing with a sander is a simple way of tackling small flat areas, especially if only part of the item needs stripping (it is hard to confine paint stripper or heat to part only). If a painted item is to be re-painted, then a light rubbing down with glasspaper is all that is needed, unless the paint is badly pitted.

**3 Using a blowtorch**
Burning the paint off with a blowtorch is a good method for metal and it will not get scorched, as tends to happen with wood. If possible work in a garage or out of doors; if indoors be very conscious of the risk of fire: have the immediate area completely bare of furnishings and furniture, and never leave a blowtorch lit and unattended. If working on a fireplace surround, strip off any wallpaper around it. Protect the floor from the falling paint, which is very hot: dampen floorboards, and, if a fitted carpet cannot be removed, cover it with dampened hardboard, not newspaper.

Do not use a blowtorch on metal window frames; the heat invariably cracks the glass. If you are using a blowtorch on cast iron, be careful not to overheat any spots as this can cause the cast iron to crack.

**4 Put it on the bonfire!**
In some cases heat can be applied by simply sticking the item in a bonfire. For example burning an old timber gate gets rid of the rotten wood but preserves any decorative metal fittings, completely free of paint.

**5 Using a hot air blower** ▽
Hot air blowers work at much lower temperatures than blowtorches and are safer, but even so use them with caution. They are less effective on metal than on wood as metal is a good conductor and dissipates the heat.

## REMOVING RUST

Whatever the original finish and the new finish you choose, it is essential to get rid of all traces of rust at this stage. Again, there are several techniques to choose from, according to the finish you want.

**1 Using a wire brush** ▽
Wire-brushing using a wire brush in a power tool is drastic treatment, suitable only for coarse, mainly flat, items such as window frames. If the rust is not very extensive a hand wire brush, or hand-sanding with emery paper will do the trick. Just brush the item first in one direction and then in another until all signs of rust have gone. Try to avoid scratching the metal more than is necessary. Steel wool will help to get the final shine.

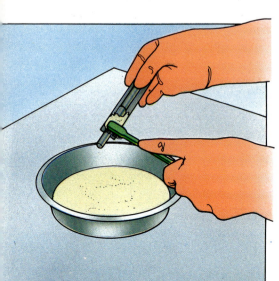

**2 Using a patent rust remover** ▽
For ornamental items with lots of curves and crevices, brush on patent rust remover; wipe or wash off following the manufacturer's instructions and allow the article to dry thoroughly before refinishing. With wrought-iron garden furniture, or anything that stands on the ground, take special care to remove all rust from underneath, as if it is left it will continue to develop under the new finish and soon spoil it.

**3 Using a special paint**
There are special paints available which are formulated to chemically de-activate the rust. If you can't find them at your DIY store, try a good car accessory shop.

First, use a wire brush to remove any loose rust. Then apply the paint, following the manufacturer's instructions. Some types act as a primer/undercoat, to be followed by any normal gloss or satin finish top coat; others are complete paint systems in one coat: Hammerite is an anti-rust primer, an undercoat and a top coat which dries quickly to a smooth or hammered metal finish.

Another system, Corroless, supplied in a two-part pack containing rust-stabilizing primer and a topcoat in a choice of six colours, uses minute heat-hardened glass flakes which leaf together to form a moisture-proof barrier. It is expensive but long lasting.

## REPAIRING DAMAGED IRONWORK

Glass fibre (or, more strictly speaking, glass fibre reinforced plastic) can be used to repair small dents or holes in iron surfaces if you are going to apply a paint finish.

**1 Choose a suitable kit**
There is a wide range of fibreglass kits available, each suitable for different types and sizes of repairs. If your local DIY store does not stock a suitable kit, try a car accessory and repair shop. Some kits include mats of glass fibre, together with resin and hardener, for a strong repair (e.g. to splits, cracks and holes in iron drainpipes or water tanks).

Kits containing glassfibre tissue are useful for giving a good finish to holes which have been repaired with mats. For small repairs, ready-mixed fibreglass is available: this consists of a paste of glass fibres and resin in a tube, together with a tube of hardener. It is suitable for making small repairs, where strength is not so important – on cast iron fire surrounds, for example.

**2 Prepare the area to be mended**
Clean the area of paint and rust first, and ensure it is thoroughly clean and dry.

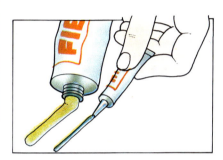

**3 Mix the ready-mix paste** △
Following the manufacturer's instructions, squeeze equal lengths of paste (containing glass fibres) and hardener on to a scrap sheet of card.

**4 Apply to the damaged ironwork** △
Use the spatula to mix the paste and hardener thoroughly. Work them together for about 30 seconds.

Spread the paste on the damaged area, and use the spatula or an old chisel or similar instrument to shape the filler to match the existing moulding or pattern. The filler will start to dry in about five minutes, so work quickly.

**5 Sand down the filled area**
Leave the filler to set hard – this will take about ten minutes. You can then sand the filler smooth if there are any irregularities.

**6 Paint over the work**
Ensure that the rest of the item is dry and free from dust and grease. Use a metal primer to paint over the surface of the bare metal and the filler, followed by undercoats and top coats as appropriate.

## FINISHES FOR IRON

**Oiling the surface** with household mineral (or easing) oil prevents the metal from rusting. Apply it with a soft cloth, working in a circular movement to ensure all the surface is covered. This finish is mainly used for tools, rather than furniture and fittings, as it rubs off on clothes.

**Applying a primer** If you want a painted finish, you will have to prime the surface (unless you use an all-in-one paint, see below). Be sure to use a metal primer, not ordinary wood primer. For iron and steel (ferrous metals) use red oxide or zinc chromate primer.

**Note** For galvanized metal use a calcium plumbate primer.

**Applying oil-based paints** Standard gloss and satin-finish oil paints are all suitable for metal. It is useful to be able to use these paints if you want to paint an item (such as a fire surround) to match the woodwork in a room. Satin black is usually used for door and window furniture and matt black for items like garden gates if preferred.

**Applying emulsion paints** Vinyl emulsions, being water based, are not suitable for painting metal. But they can be applied to radiators if desired to match the wall, provided these have a perfect factory paint finish.

**Radiator enamel** This is an acrylic paint which is baked on to the surface by turning the radiator on immediately after application. Radiators can also be finished with gloss or satin oil paint, but allow them to harden before heating up again or they may blister.

**Heat-resisting enamels** These give a more durable finish for radiators, and are suitable for items which get hot – such as boiler cabinets and cookers.

**Heatproof enamels** These stand up to the very high temperatures reached on fire grates or ranges actually being used – usually sold as stove black.

**Metallic paints** These rust-resisting paints dry to a glossy finish with either a hammered or crazed appearance. They are very tough, also heat resistant, and come in a range of colours. Only one coat is required; no primer or undercoat. They are useful for exterior metalwork, and for re-finishing metal furniture.

**Black lead** (grate polish) Housemaids in Victorian days used this to smarten up fireplace surrounds and grates, and it is still available. It is a black cream which is applied with a soft cloth (use a toothbrush for crevices) and then buffed with another cloth to build up a soft, silvery shine and moisture-proof finish. As it contains carbon, take care not to get any polish on surrounding wallpaper or woodwork.

## MAINTAINING IRON AND STEEL

When these metals are painted, no maintenance is required beyond normal dusting or an occasional wipe with a damp cloth. But keep an eye on painted metals for signs of any breakdown in the paint film, as once this happens the way is open for moisture to get in and rust to build up. A light rub down and a fresh coat of paint may be all that is necessary if you act quickly.

**1 Oiling polished metals**
Metals which have been oiled should be re-treated from time to time. Rub down with emery paper if there are any traces of rust, then apply mineral oil as before. Work in a circular movement so that all the surface is covered.

**2 Care of kitchen utensils**
Clean carbon steel knife blades with scouring powder, and dry thoroughly. To prevent cast iron frying pans and woks from rusting, dry thoroughly after washing and then put them on a warm radiator or in a hot oven. If you are not going to use them for some time, rub them over with cooking oil to prevent rust forming.

**3 Using black lead**
To maintain a silvery finish on stripped cast iron fire surrounds, polish as regularly as possible with black lead (grate polish). It comes in a tube, and contains carbon and graphite, which together give an almost pewter-like finish, and is available from most good fireplace stockists or hardware stores. If you are polishing a fireplace which is made totally of iron, without a wooden surround, hold a large piece of card against the wall at the edge of the fire surround to prevent the blacklead marking the wall.

### BRIGHT IDEA

**A tip for fingers** To clean carbon steel knife blades with no fear of cutting your fingers, use a cork. Place the knife flat on a draining board and dip an ordinary wine cork in water, then scouring powder. Rub the flat end on the blade of the knife, like a scourer.

◁ **Bright lights**
This old cast iron conservatory light has been given a new lease of life with a coat of specially formulated paint. The Corroless paint system consists of an undercoat and topcoat (available in six different colours). The fire surround has also been painted – you should use stove black in a situation where the paint will be exposed to heat.

# RENOVATING BRASS, COPPER OR BRONZE

Brass, copper and bronze are useful and decorative. Treat them with care and they will last for centuries.

Proper treatment and regular polishing of brass and copper will keep them looking warm and bright. The treatments needed depend on the age and condition of the item and the finished effect that you want to achieve. A polished finish is one of the most popular, and this can be protected with lacquer to save on housework. In some situations, you may need to paint these metals (particularly copper). If so, it is essential to use the correct type of primer to ensure the paint adheres and you get a lasting finish.

## USES FOR COPPER, BRASS AND BRONZE

Traditionally, brass had many functional uses in the home. Because it is durable and does not rust it was used for taps, stop cocks and other plumbing fittings. Indeed, most modern taps are still made from brass, but they are chrome plated so that you don't continually have to polish the brass. Now, brass taps are making a come-back, particularly in period-style homes, where fittings are chosen to be decorative as well as functional.

Another frequent use for brass is as door furniture, on both old and new houses. On older houses knobs and knockers may have been painted over, often to save on cleaning.

Brass fire irons and coal scuttles are also traditional, and you may well pick up brass desk accessories and clocks. Such items as candlesticks, light fittings and horse brasses have never lost their appeal.

A particularly attractive use for brass is in bedsteads – and you may find small areas of brass on other furniture, such as drawer handles, decorative plates, cupboard keyholes and so on.

The main use for copper in modern homes is in central heating pipes. Traditionally, it has uses in the kitchen: copper bowls for beating egg whites, copper pans (and copper-bottomed pans) and jelly moulds, for example. Any copper cooking utensils should be lined with tin, particularly if they are to be used for mixing acid ingredients.

You may also find decorative accessories (lamps, plant troughs and so on) made either from copper or a mixture of copper and brass.

## WHAT IS IT MADE OF?

**Copper** is a pure metal which is easy to bend and shape. It is easily recognizable when untarnished by its attractive reddish-brown colour; exposure to damp causes it to develop a green deposit called verdigris (hence grey-green copper-clad church spires).

**Brass** is made by mixing copper with 20-40 per cent zinc (another pure metal). New or well-polished brass gleams like gold; exposure to air causes it to darken to the point where it is almost unrecognizable.

**Bronze** is another alloy of copper, this time with the addition of 10 per cent tin. It does not have any common functional uses in the home, but you may find bronze statuettes or other ornaments. Traditionally, it is allowed to tarnish to a deep golden brown: the patina (or tarnish) is considered part of its charm.

*Fresh French style*
*New or old, brass sets the style in a bedroom. New brass is usually lacquered, and needs a minimum amount of care. Unlacquered brass should be polished regularly. Brass can be painted with enamel paint or oil-based gloss with a suitable undercoat. Pretty floral bedlinen completes the traditional look.*

### CHECK YOUR NEEDS

**For cleaning tarnished copper and brass:**
- ☐ Salt and vinegar OR
- ☐ Washing soda OR
- ☐ Lemon and salt

**For cleaning small brass items:**
- ☐ Plastic container
- ☐ Tin foil and string
- ☐ Washing soda

**For removing old finishes:**
- ☐ Paint stripper
- ☐ Old paint brush
- ☐ Toothbrush (optional)
- ☐ Rubber gloves

**For re-lacquering**
- ☐ Paint stripper
- ☐ Spray-on metal lacquer OR
- ☐ Metal lacquer
- ☐ New, artist's soft paintbrush

**For painting:**
- ☐ Zinc chromate primer
- ☐ Undercoat, topcoat
- ☐ Paint brushes

**For maintaining a shine:**
- ☐ Soft cloth
- ☐ Appropriate polish OR
- ☐ Vinegar
- ☐ Oatmeal
- ☐ Masking tape (if cleaning *in situ*)

### RENOVATING COPPER AND BRASS

Copper which has been exposed to heat and fumes – for example, old cooking utensils – and brass which has been neglected may have turned quite black. Renovation requires the use of a weak acid plus abrasive. The following are cheaper than proprietary cleaners.

**1** *Gentle scouring* △
A cheap and effective method is to scour the item with a mixture of neat vinegar and salt. Dip a sponge in the mixture and rub on the item.

**2** *Soaking in washing soda*
An alternative is to fill the sink with boiling water, add a cupful of washing soda and soak the item overnight. Try removing any remaining corrosion with a flat scourer and non-scratch cream; resort to scouring powder only if necessary.

**3** *Lemon and salt* △
Items which are relatively lightly tarnished can be rubbed with a cut lemon dipped in coarse salt.

**4** *The last resort*
Using a harsh abrasive risks scratching the metal, but in really bad cases you may have to resort to a nylon pad, and scouring powder where necessary. Rinse in warm water and dry immediately or it will darken again.

### USING WASHING SODA

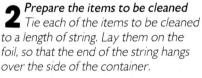

**1** *Prepare a container* △
For small items such as brass door knobs, door and drawer handles and escutcheons a variation of the washing soda technique is useful. Line a plastic container with cooking foil.

**2** *Prepare the items to be cleaned*
Tie each of the items to be cleaned to a length of string. Lay them on the foil, so that the end of the string hangs over the side of the container.

**3** *Add the solution* △
Dissolve a cup of washing soda in four pints of very hot water and pour the solution into the bowl. It will fizz and bubble up. Leave for a few minutes, then lift out a knob by the string and see if it is clean; replace if necessary. Rinse and dry.

### STRIPPING PAINT FROM COPPER, BRASS AND BRONZE

A conventional, liquid paint stripper, normally used for stripping paint from woodwork, can be used for this. Although the newer, paste strippers are generally considered to be more efficient, they blacken these metals.

**1** *Prepare the item to be stripped*
Remove door furniture which is painted or, for larger items (e.g. bedsteads), stand them in the middle of the room on newspaper with all other surfaces well protected – or take them out of doors.

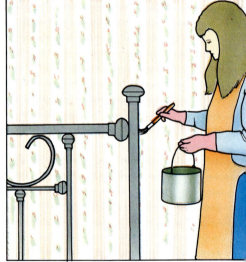

**2** *Apply the stripper* △
Use an old paintbrush to apply a liberal coat of stripper, following the manufacturer's instructions. Leave for 20 minutes, to let the chemicals take effect. For small items, pour the stripper into a metal or ceramic container and dip the items to be stripped into it, repeating until they are clean.

**3 Check the progress** △
Use a paint scraper to lift off the stripper and softened paint and check that the stripper has worked right through all the layers of paint. Following the manufacturer's instructions, apply more stripper if necessary.

**4 Remove the paint**
Use a paint scraper to lift off all the stripper and paint. Use an old toothbrush to work the softened paint out of corners. Finally, wash the items thoroughly to remove all traces of stripper.

## APPLYING A NEW LACQUER FINISH
Modern brass door furniture and decorative accessories are usually clear lacquered so they need no polishing, but with time this breaks down, moisture gets underneath and the metal darkens.

**1 Clean off existing lacquer**
Remove the items and strip the lacquer off with liquid paint stripper; do not use paste stripper which will turn the brass black; or abrasive methods which would scratch it.

**2 Apply the new lacquer**
Use a clear metal lacquer rather than polyurethane; this can be obtained in liquid or spray-on form. Work in a warm room, or the lacquer may go cloudy, and make every effort to banish dust beforehand. Use a new, dust-free artists' brush if painting.

## FINISHES FOR COPPER, BRASS AND BRONZE
**Polished finish** Once cleaned up, copper, brass and bronze can be left as they are, and simply polished or buffed up from time to time.
**Lacquered finish** Special lacquers are available, which allow the colour of the metal to show through (see above).
**Paint** In some situations you may want to paint these metals. New central heating pipes, for example, can look lovely, but keeping the shine is a nuisance. Before painting, clean off tarnish and any grease with fine steel wool dipped in white spirit, then prime with an all-purpose primer or zinc chromate primer before undercoating and top coating. If you are using emulsion paint, primer is unnecessary.

## MAINTENANCE
Once cleaned up, if you are not applying lacquer, keep brass and copper clean by regular polishing with a proprietary metal polish.
**Liquid brass polish** is best for items with a lot of detail, as it can be worked in with a toothbrush; but it can also be hard to remove.
**Impregnated wadding** is convenient to use, and good for smooth items.
**Heavy-duty polish** in a tube is available for neglected copper.
**Powders** are also available for cleaning metals. They are either mixed to a paste, applied and then polished off when dry, or you can dip a damp cloth in the powder, clean the item, and then rinse and dry it.

## TRADITIONAL BRASS CLEANER
Brass can also be cleaned using two items you probably have ready to hand in the kitchen: vinegar and porridge oats or oatmeal. This method has been used by the Portuguese for generations.

**1 Mix a paste**
Mix 3-4 tablespoons of the oats with enough vinegar to form a thick paste.

**2 Apply the paste**
Spread the paste over the item with your hands, working it well in to any decorated or indented areas.

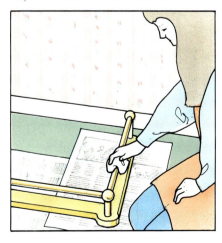

**3 Polish up the brass** △
Leave to dry for a few minutes, then wipe off with a soft cloth.

## CLEANING HANDLES IN SITU

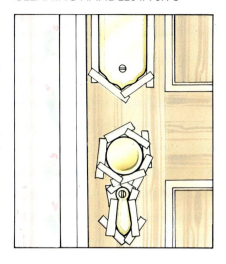

Cleaning brass door furniture or cabinet fittings *in situ* is very difficult to do effectively and without damaging surrounding paintwork or wood. For a really thorough clean it is well worth unscrewing the fittings. Otherwise protect the surrounding area with strips of masking tape. Do not press the tape in place too firmly, and lift it gently when you have finished polishing, to avoid damaging the paintwork or polish. Polish up wood after cleaning the door furniture – wax will not harm the brass.

## RENOVATION AND MAINTENANCE OF BRONZE
Bronze requires slightly different treatment to copper and brass, as part of its attraction lies in the depth of colour of the patina (the brownish green coating it develops as it oxidizes).

**1 Remove verdigris**
Bronze should not need much attention, unless it has been left out of doors and allowed to get badly corroded. Encrustations of verdigris can be treated with a mixture of nine parts water and one part vinegar: dip a sponge in the mixture and wipe over the item, then dry thoroughly.

**2 Maintain the patina**
Once clean, bronze items should just be dusted and rubbed up with a soft cloth. Never polish them.

**3 Wash occasionally**
If bronze ornaments are in a room where they get a build-up of greasy dirt (in a kitchen, or open-plan living room, for example) you can wash them occasionally in hot water with a mild detergent.

△ **A welcome by the hearthside**
The brass coal scuttle and fender make a welcoming sight. Well polished, they reflect the flickering flames, and create a warm glow even when the fire is not lit. Brass candlesticks add a formal touch to the mantelpiece.

▷ **Copper bottoms**
In the kitchen, copper pans are both functional and decorative, Here, bowls for beating egg whites and small pans are displayed on a traditional iron rack, which can be fixed to the wall close to the cooker.

## BRIGHT IDEA

**DISTRESSING EFFECTS**

Old brass and copper ware is readily identifiable by the dents and scratches acquired over the years, and a mellow colour. Modern brass or copper ware can be 'distressed' in the same way as is done with some reproduction furniture, to remove its brash newness.

To produce dents, lightly hammer the item with the rounded end of a ball-pein hammer (a small hammer with a ball on one side of the head), or a tack hammer protected with a bit of leather. Rubbing dirt (earth or boot polish) into the crevices completes the deception.

The colour can be changed with chemicals which you may be able to obtain from chemists; handle with care and avoid skin or eye contact. Soaking in a weak solution of ammonium sulphide will deepen and enrich the red tones in both copper and brass. Rinse and dry thoroughly.

To give brass an antique green tinge use a solution of 100 grams of copper nitrate dissolved in 100 ml of water. Heat the solution to 60°C (140°F) and brush over the item every few hours, then leave overnight. Rinse and dry.

# LAYING CORK AND VINYL FLOOR TILES

Laying cork or vinyl tiles is one of the easiest ways of providing a durable and stylish floorcovering

Cork and vinyl make practical floors for hard-wear areas such as kitchens and bathrooms. They can also be used imaginatively in other rooms too: in living and dining rooms, for example, a neutral-coloured background of tiles is an excellent foil for colourful rugs.

Laying tiles is relatively simple: they are light and easier to handle than sheet flooring, and there's usually less wastage involved if you make a mistake in cutting to size. Tiles can also be used to create interesting floor designs by mixing colours or plain and patterned tiles.

## CORK OR VINYL?

The appearance of the floorcovering is important, of course, but cork and vinyl each have their own qualities.

**Cork** has an attractive natural look and it is comfortable, warm and quiet to walk on.

Colours range from a warm honey-gold to dark chocolate brown. Most tiles are plain, but some are patterned with geometric designs in contrasting cork, while others are marbled with touches of colour, such as green or red.

Tiles are available with different finishes: they can be pre-sealed with a clear acrylic or vinyl coating for increased durability; or pre-waxed; or left untreated (these are usually called 'pre-sanded').

Untreated cork must be sealed after laying with polyurethane varnish or special floor sealant to give a tough wipe-down finish. Pre-sealed tiles also benefit from one or two extra coatings of seal to prevent water seeping into joins between tiles.

**Vinyl** is harder wearing than cork but a little less gentle on the feet. Some vinyls, however, are 'cushioned' with a layer of foam to make them softer to walk on.

Tiles come in a wide range of colours and patterns, and are available with a smooth surface or with an embossed and textured finish to look like natural brick or stone.

Some brands have a self-adhesive backing, which makes the job of laying them a lot simpler.

**Care and maintenance** Vinyl and sealed cork tiles have an easy-clean surface. Simply wipe with a well-wrung cloth or mop. To remove grease or stubborn dirt, use a little washing-up liquid; do not use harsh abrasive detergents.

Pre-waxed cork tiles should be polished occasionally.

## BUYING TILES

Most cork and vinyl tiles are 300mm (about 1ft) square and are usually sold in packs sufficient to cover about one square metre. To calculate how many tiles you need, see overleaf.

Always store bought tiles flat. Cork tiles must be taken out of their wrapping and left in the room in which they are to be laid for at least 24 hours before laying. As the colour can vary slightly from pack to pack, it is a good idea to mix all the tiles up before laying.

*Natural looks*
*Natural cork is an attractive and practical choice for halls and children's rooms, for example, as well as kitchens and bathrooms – warm, safe and quickly mopped or wiped clean.*

## SURFACE PREPRATION

Tiles must be laid on a sound, dry and level sub-floor – otherwise they will crack and wear badly.

Cover floorboards with sheets of hardboard to make a level surface.

Slight irregularities in a solid sub-floor (concrete, for example) can be levelled with a self-smoothing compound, but a badly damaged floor should be dealt with by professionals.

Existing tiled or sheet flooring can usually be tiled over as long as it is in good condition and firmly fixed in place: check manufacturer's instructions before buying new tiles to see if this is recommended.

Before laying hardboard or new tiles make sure that the door will clear the extra thickness – see Step 7.

## TOOLS AND EQUIPMENT

**Hardboard** to cover uneven floorboards. Buy sheets of standard hardboard, 3.2mm thick, plus hardboard pins to fix them.

**Self-levelling screed compound** is used to level off a rough or uneven solid floor of concrete, stone or brick. It comes ready-mixed in tubs, or in powder form to be mixed with water. A 10kg bag of powder covers about 50sq m of floor.

**Screeding mortar** is used to fill any holes in a solid floor before levelling. It is available ready-mixed.

**Cork flooring adhesive** comes ready-mixed in tubs and a notched spreader is usually supplied. One litre covers about 3sq m.

Use a non-flammable emulsion adhesive, not a solvent-based one.

**Vinyl tile adhesive** – unless you're laying self-adhesive tiles, use a ready-mixed emulsion-type flooring adhesive. Allow about 1 litre of adhesive per 4-6sq m. Apply with a notched spreader.

**A profile gauge** – a device like a comb with sliding teeth – makes it easier to cut tiles to fit awkward shapes such as door architraves. Otherwise, cut a template from card or paper.

**Polyurethane varnish or floor sealant** to seal untreated cork tiles. These are available in matt, semi-gloss or gloss finishes.

Two or three coats are needed as the first coat tends to sink into the cork and look patchy. One litre of varnish covers about 5sq m on the first coat, and about 15sq m on second or third coats.

## CALCULATING QUANTITIES

Once you know the tile size, you can calculate how many tiles you need:

**Measure the length** of the area to be tiled and divide it by the tile size to give the number of tiles needed to fit in one row. Count part tiles as whole tiles.

**Measure the width** of the area to be covered and divide this by the tile size. Count part tiles as whole ones.

**Multiply** the two figures together to get the total number of tiles needed.

Buy a few extra tiles to allow for any mistakes in cutting. You can always use them to repair worn or damaged patches later.

## TILE PATTERNS

If you're going to make a pattern with tiles of different colour or design, make a scale drawing of the room on graph paper and mark in the pattern. Then count up how many tiles of each colour or design you will need.

When laying the tiles, keep your plan handy to make sure that you are following it correctly.

## CHECK YOUR NEEDS

- ☐ Tiles
- ☐ String
- ☐ Chalk
- ☐ Pencil or felt-tipped marker
- ☐ Adhesive
- ☐ Notched adhesive spreader
- ☐ Cutting board (eg, an offcut of hardboard or chipboard)
- ☐ Sharp craft knife and blades
- ☐ Metal rule
- ☐ Profile gauge OR card or paper for templates

### For untreated cork tiles:
- ☐ Polyurethane varnish
- ☐ 75 or 100mm paintbrush
- ☐ Steel wool – fine and medium
- ☐ White spirit

### For levelling wooden floors:
- ☐ Hardboard – 3.2mm thick
- ☐ Panel saw or jigsaw
- ☐ Hammer and nail punch
- ☐ 25mm hardboard pins

### For levelling solid floors:
- ☐ Screeding mortar (optional)
- ☐ Self levelling screed compound
- ☐ Plastic bucket
- ☐ Steel float

## PREPARING THE SURFACE

The sub-floor must be structurally sound, smooth and level, and free of dust and grease.

### Scrub down old flooring

If existing tiles or wood blocks are flat and firmly fixed, they can often be left in place and tiled over.

Scrub the floor with a solution of warm water and sugar soap or household detergent to remove dirt, and rinse. Then rough up the surface with medium-grade steel wool to give a key for new tile adhesive

### Level a wooden floor

*Prepare the floor by punching in any protruding nails with a hammer and nail punch, and secure loose boards with nails or screws. Then sweep the floor and cover the whole surface with sheets of hardboard.*

*Lay the sheets rough side up, with 3mm between each sheet to allow for expansion. To fill gaps round edges of the room, cut sheets to size, sawing with the rough side down. Don't worry about fitting them exactly to contours of the wall. Fix securely with hardboard pins nailed all over at 15cm intervals.*

### Level a solid floor ▷

*Fill any holes and small cracks with screed mortar; sweep the floor and wash down with detergent solution. Then use a self-levelling screed compound to level the floor.*

*Starting at the furthest point from the door, pour some compound on to the floor. Use a steel float, held at a slight angle, to spread it evenly to a thickness of about 3mm. Cover the whole floor (making sure that you finish up at the door) and leave to smooth itself out.*

*Do not fix new tiles until the compound has hardened completely – this can take up to 12 hours.*

## LAYING THE TILES

A tiled floor looks best if you start tiling from the middle of the room so that any cut tiles are around the edges of the room.

It is worth making a trial layout of tiles first to check how they fit. You can then adjust the starting point a little, if necessary, so that you have at least a third or half a tile's width left at the edges – this makes accurate cutting and shaping to fit much easier.

### 1 Find the centre point ▷
Mark the midpoint of two opposite walls, then stretch a length of string between the two points and pin it to the skirting boards. Repeat for the other two facing walls. The centre point is where the strings cross.

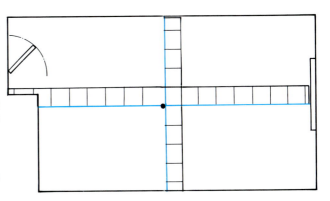

### 2 Check the fit ▷
Starting from the centre point, lay a row of loose tiles (without adhesive) out towards each wall. Butt the tiles up closely and keep them hard against the string lines.

If the space between the end of a row of tiles and the wall is very narrow, adjust the string a little and shift the tiles so that the gap is at least a third of a tile wide. In the diagram, for example, moving the tiles to the left a little reduces the amount of fiddly cutting along the door wall and leaves whole tiles on the window wall.

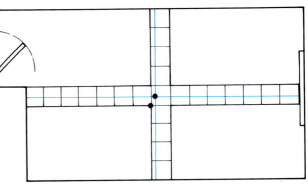

### 3 Mark the floor
When you're satisfied with the layout, lift the tiles. Then rub each length of string with chalk and snap it against the floor to leave chalked guidelines to follow when laying the tiles.

Remove the strings but leave the pins in place so that chalked marks can be remade if necessary.

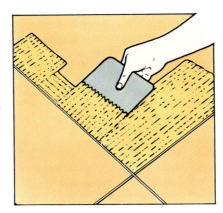

### 4 Spread the adhesive △
Start in the quarter of the room furthest from the door. Work away from the centre point out along the chalk lines, and apply only as much adhesive as is necessary for laying about four tiles at a time.

Fixing methods and adhesives vary so follow manufacturer's instructions. With some tiles, for example, you have to spread adhesive on the underside of the tile as well as on the floor.

### 5 Stick the first tile down △
The position of the first tile is all important. Place it at the centre point, aligning it carefully inside the angle of the chalk guidelines. Then press it down firmly on top of the adhesive with the palm of your hand.

### Untreated cork tiles
Make sure you lay untreated cork tiles rough side down.

As they mark very easily, protect the surface with polythene or dust sheets and kneel on a board to spread your weight while you work. Don't kneel on newspaper – your weight will transfer indelible ink on to the cork.

### 6 Tile the first quarter ◁
Stick the tiles down, working in a fan shape outwards from the centre point. Butt the tiles against each other, lowering them carefully into place rather than sliding them on the floor. Use a damp cloth to remove any adhesive squeezed up between tiles before it sets.

Finish laying whole tiles, then move on to the next quarter. Leave cut border tiles until last.

### 7 Tile the other quarters
Tile the other three quarters of the room in the same way as the first, leaving the section by the door until last so that you don't disturb tiles already laid.

Before you lay tiles in the door area, check that the extra thickness of the tiles fits in the gap under the door – you may have to remove the door and plane down its bottom edge so that it clears the newly laid tiles.

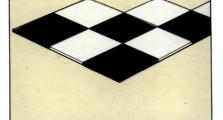

  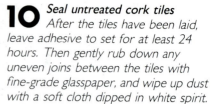

**8** *Mark out border tiles* △
When you have laid all the whole tiles, start filling in the gaps round the edges of the room.

Place the tile to be cut squarely on top of the last whole tile laid before the skirting board. Place another whole tile on top but with its edge pressed firmly against the skirting. Draw a cutting line across the middle tile with a sharp pencil, using the top one as a profile – the exposed part of the middle tile should fit the gap exactly.

## CUTTING CORNER TILES ▷

Use the same technique as for borders, but position the tile to be cut on both sides of the angle and mark the tile with two cutting lines.

Join up the pencil lines and cut away the waste to leave an L-shaped filler piece.

### Vinyl check ▽

Vinyl tiles in two or more colours can be used to create interesting floor patterns such as this smart black-and-white check, but careful planning on graph paper is essential.

**9** *Cut border tiles* △
Place the marked tile on a cutting board. Place a metal rule against the pencil line, and cut the tile carefully with a sharp knife. Make sure you change the blade of your trimming knife whenever it starts to feel blunt so that you always get a clean cut right through the tile.

Try the cut tile for size and trim if necessary. Then spread the adhesive on to the surface and press the cut tile into place.

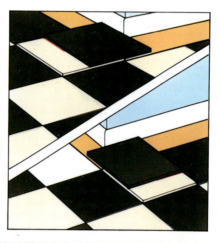

**10** *Seal untreated cork tiles*
After the tiles have been laid, leave adhesive to set for at least 24 hours. Then gently rub down any uneven joins between the tiles with fine-grade glasspaper, and wipe up dust with a soft cloth dipped in white spirit.

Pour some polyurethane varnish into a wide-necked container so that you can use a large paintbrush easily. Then, starting in the corner farthest from the door, apply two or three coats of varnish. Allow plenty of time for each coat to dry, and rub the surface with very fine wire wool between coats to key it.

Leave the varnish to harden for two or three days before replacing furniture.

**11** *Fit threshold strips*
Protect the raw edges of tiles in doorways by fitting a metal or wooden threshold strip across the opening.

## CUTTING AWKWARD SHAPES △

Use a card or paper template, or a profile gauge, to mark tiles to fit round objects such as pipes, mouldings or door architrave.

A profile gauge is useful when dealing with intricate shapes – push the metal teeth firmly against the object and mark the impression on the tile. Then cut it out carefully with a craft knife or sharp scissors (for vinyl tiles).

**Conceal gaps** Hide slight gaps round the edges by nailing lengths of 12mm quadrant beading into the angle between skirting and floor. Then paint the beading to match the skirting.

# LAYING SHEET FLOORING

Sheet flooring can be trickier to lay than tiles, but gives a beautiful seam-free finish in all but the largest rooms.

Smooth sheet floorings are ideal for kitchens and bathrooms, where spills occur and easy cleaning is essential. They are also popular for halls and kid's rooms where wet feet, muddy pets, and accidents can be dealt with quickly.

Sheet floorings are fitted wall-to-wall. This is useful in small bathrooms, where water spills on the floor and seeps between tile joints, causing them to lift, prompting rotten floorboards and damage to the ceiling below. Sheet floorings are quicker to lay than tiles, as they don't have to be stuck down all over; indeed, 'lay-flat' types can be loose-laid after trimming. However, manipulating the sheet into position can be tricky, so for your first attempt lay a cheap material in a small area.

## TYPES OF SHEET FLOORING

**Sheet vinyl** is the most common material around, and comes in two main varieties. Unbacked vinyls are made by sandwiching a PVC pattern between a clear protective surface and solid vinyl. The surface may be smooth or textured to match the printed pattern – with grout lines on a tiled pattern, or wood grain on a simulated timber one.

Cushioned or backed vinyls, have an extra layer of foam between the patterned layer and the backing, making them soft and warm underfoot. Some of the brick and marble imitations available are remarkably realistic.

**Linoleum** is a tough natural material and is no longer as brittle as it used to be. It can be loose laid on concrete or hardboard. More expensive than vinyl.

**Rubber flooring** comes in strong colours, in plain or three-dimensional finishes – such as ribs, studs and squares. It is durable and studded types are non-slip. It is more expensive than vinyl.

## PREPARING THE SUB-FLOOR

Whether you're laying sheet vinyl, lino or rubber, the floor preparation is the same. All can be laid on solid concrete or suspended timber floors. Preparing the floor properly is important, a bad job brings poor results. You should:

☐ Lift existing floorcoverings (well-stuck tiles can be left in place, as can sheet materials that have been firmly stuck down all over, if the surface is smooth and even).
☐ Drive in nails on boarded floors.
☐ Put down a hardboard underlay if boarded floors are gappy or uneven.
☐ Seal dusty concrete floors with diluted PVA bonding agent.
☐ Apply a self-smoothing compound if concrete floors are uneven or pitted. See page 68.

*Tile effect*
*This cushioned vinyl flooring gives the impression of a traditional stone floor with inlaid tiles, but it is easy to clean, soft and warm underfoot.*

## ESTIMATING QUANTITIES

Sheet floorings are usually sold in 2m and 4m widths although you may find some brands in 3m widths. They are sold by the linear metre. Choose a width that will cover the floor without seams if possible; obviously these will be unavoidable in rooms more than 4m wide, and in L-shaped rooms, The best way of estimating your needs (and minimizing unnecessary and expensive waste) is to draw a floor plan of the room, complete with alcoves and other irregularities (see right).

Work to a scale of say 1:50 which means measurements taken in mm should be divided by 50, so two large squares on the floor plan equal one metre. Make sure all dimensions are marked on the plan and take it to your supplier for advice on the best choice of cut.

## TOOLS AND EQUIPMENT

There are no special tools or equipment required for laying sheet flooring. You do need a scribing block for marking a line on the flooring before cutting but you can make this yourself. It is used to mark the longest straight edge of the sheet so it fits neatly against the skirting board. It can also be used for drawing around obstacles such as pedestals. All you need is a piece of scrap wood about 50×25mm in cross-section and around 300mm long. Drill a hole through it about 50mm from one end, making sure it is large enough to accept a ball-point pen.

### CHECK YOUR NEEDS
**For levelling wooden sub-floors:**
☐ Hardboard – 3mm thick
☐ Panel saw or power jigsaw
☐ Hammer and nail punch
☐ 25mm hardboard pins

**For levelling concrete floors:**
☐ Self-smoothing compound
☐ Plastic bucket
☐ Steel float
☐ Sheet floorcovering
☐ Tape measure

☐ Metal rule
☐ Craft knife and spare blades
☐ Scribing block and ballpoint pen (or a pair of compasses)
☐ Profile gauge
☐ Flooring adhesive or heavy duty double sided tape
☐ Notched spreader (for adhesive)
☐ Door threshold strip
☐ Screws (for threshold strip)
☐ Scissors
☐ Seam roller

## LAYING THE FLOORCOVERING

Unlike tiles, sheet flooring doesn't need much planning before you start laying. Your main aim is to avoid having seams in areas of heavy wear such as doorways, and to align the pattern so that it runs parallel with the longest straight wall in the room. When your flooring supplier has looked at your scale plan he should be able to tell you which way to lay your length.

Note that some sheet floorings have a definite selvedge along each side of the length; this has to be trimmed off at edges or when butt joints are made between lengths. Ask about this when buying the flooring and remember to allow for this if your room width closely matches the width of the material you're laying.

**1 Prepare the surface**
Clear the room of furniture and prepare the floor surface as necessary (see page 68). Then leave the new flooring in the room where it is to be laid for 48 hours to acclimatize; it's best to unroll it when it's delivered and either lay it out flat (with a fold or two across the width) or roll it up again loosely and stand it on its end.

**2 Scribe the edge ▷**
Unroll the sheet parallel with the longest straight wall in the room, and push up one edge against the skirting board. Let the other edges lap up the other walls at this stage. Then slide the length away from the skirting by about 25mm, and position your scribing block on it with the end holding the pen nearest the skirting. Keep this end pushed firmly against the skirting, and with your left hand holding the pen and your right hand gripping the block draw the block towards you so the pen scribes the profile of the skirting on the sheet.

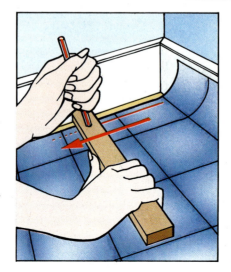

**3 Cut the edge**
Using a craft knife cut along the scribed line, following it as closely as possible, and discard the offcut. Now slide the sheet back against the wall to check its fit. Trim locally as necessary.

**4 Trim the waste**
If there is more than about 50mm of waste riding up the skirting boards along the other three walls, trim it off roughly to leave about 50mm all round ready for the final trimming (see step 6). Make sure you leave enough waste material across door openings to allow the floorcovering to reach to the position of the threshold strip.

**5** *Cut internal corners* ▽
Next, make cuts into the waste at an angle of 45 degrees at all internal corners to allow the rest of the sheet to lie flat. Do this in stages, so you don't cut too far in. You can't put it back if you make a mistake.

**6** *Cut external corners* ▽
Approach external corners with care. At a chimney breast, for example, press the sheet into the angle across the face of the breast wall, fold the surplus back and mark the position of each external corner on the underside of the sheet. Then cut in from the waste edge of the sheet towards this mark at an angle of about 45 degrees, extending the cut until the sheet lies flat round the corner with the waste material lapping up the skirting on each side. It's easy to make mistakes, so think before cutting.

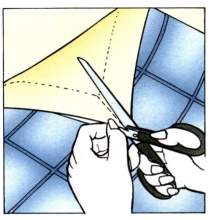
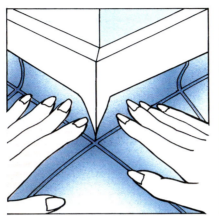
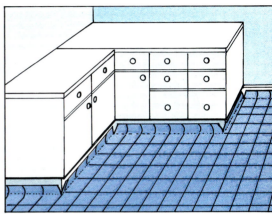

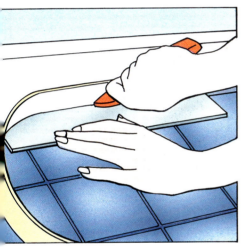

**7** *The final trimming* ◁
When the flooring is lying flat, it is time to do the final trimming round the rest of the room. First trim a side adjacent to the scribed edge. Start at one end of the wall you scribed earlier, and with your metal rule, press the sheet into the floor/skirting angle. Then push the knife blade through the sheet and draw it along the metal rule, holding the knife against the skirting to follow the floor/skirting profile. Trim in this way to remove waste from other edges. Check that the flooring fits all round, make further cuts if necessary.

**8** *Cutting awkward shapes*
At awkward obstacles, such as door architraves, use a profile gauge to take an impression of the architrave's profile and use this to mark and cut the sheet to fit (see page 70).

Where central heating pipes rise through the floor, make a short right-angled cut in from the edge of the sheet in line with one side of the pipe and then trim out a circle to match the pipe diameter. If you have overcut edges, disguise the gap by pinning lengths of slim beading to the bottom of the skirting board and paint.

**9** *Joining lengths* ▽
In very wide rooms, you can't avoid having a seam across the room between two lengths of flooring. Lay the first length as described along one half of the room. Then lay the second length parallel to it, and overlap the edges so you can align the pattern carefully. Tape the two lengths together temporarily with adhesive tape laid across the join, and cut through both layers with your knife and metal rule (far left). Remove the two offcut strips and check that the edges meet neatly and match correctly (left).

Then slide the second length back out of the way and fold back the meeting edge of the first (fitted) length. Stick a strip of double-sided tape to the floor beneath the joint line and peel off the paper. Bed the edge of the first length on to it, realign the cut edge of the second length with it, matching the pattern accurately (right). Then, stick it down well with a seam roller (far right). You can then trim the other three edges of the second length as described.

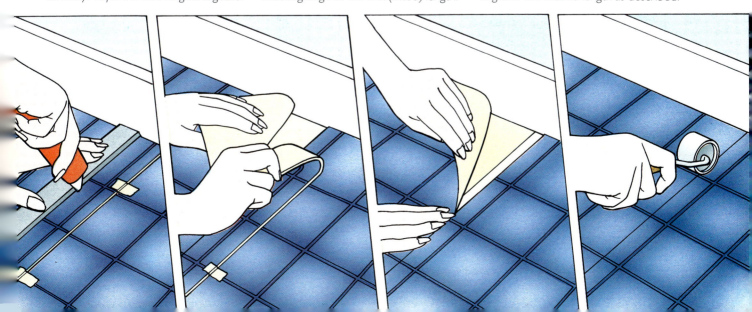

**10** *Cutting around obstacles* ▽
In bathrooms and WCs you may be faced with the problem of having to cut round basin and WC pedestals. The best way of coping with these is to make a paper template and to cut the entire sheet on the floor elsewhere in the house.

Tape sheets of paper to the floor of the room you're fitting and to each other, so that their edges are about 25mm in from the skirting all round.

Use a craft knife to cut the sheets so that they fit roughly round pedestals and other obstacles (left). Then use your scribing block (see Step 2) to draw the room outline (and the outline of any obstacles) on the paper (centre).

Now lift the template, lay it on to the unrolled floorcovering in another room and reverse the scribing procedure. Let the end of the block follow the line on the template, and the pen will trace out the room's outline on the vinyl (right). It may be easier to do this with a pair of compasses (set to match the distance between the end of the block and the pen tip). You can then cut along the outline with a knife or scissors (easier on curves) and discard the waste.

If you are cutting round a pedestal base, make a straight cut in from the edge of the sheet, so that you can slide the two 'tongues' behind the pedestal. If you carried out the two scribing stages carefully, you should get a perfect fit.

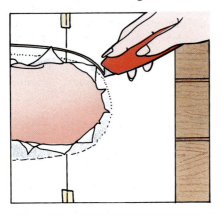
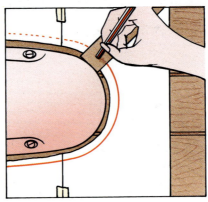
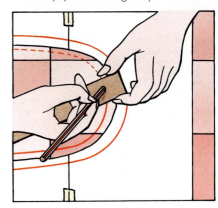

**11** *Securing the edges* ▷
All that remains is to stick down the edges of the sheet (this isn't necessary with some 'lay-flat' brands) and to fit a threshold strip across the doorway if there isn't one there already.

Use either flooring adhesive or double-sided tape for the edges. Lift back each edge in turn and spread adhesive or bed tape on the floor surface. Then press the edge down firmly all the way along. Repeat the process for the other edges of the room.

Finally, at the doorway (right) tuck the edge of the sheet under the threshold strip. You may have to lift the old one and fit a new one if the previous floorcovering was carpet as the jaws of the strip are likely to be too wide and could pose a trip hazard.

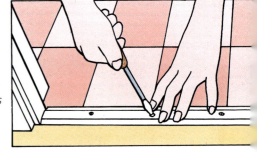

### MAINTENANCE
Before cleaning your floor study the manufacturer's instructions.
**Vinyl flooring** Sweep or damp-mop daily. Wash regularly with a cloth, wrung out in soapy water. Polish with self-shine finish or floor cleaner/polisher.
**Linoleum** Sweep, dry-mop or wipe over with a cloth, wrung out in soapy water. Polish with wax, self-shine polish or floor cleaner/polisher.
**Rubber** Sweep or damp-mop. Apply self-shine polish weekly until the flooring is non-absorbent. Wash if dirty.

### WORDS OF CAUTION
☐ Never place hot objects on vinyl – they can damage it. Similarly corrosive liquids such as paint-stripper leave marks.
☐ Never lay sheet flooring near solid fuel fires or boilers – heat discolours flooring.
☐ Mats laid on sheet flooring need a non-slip backing.

### BRIGHT IDEA

Take advantage of the waterproof nature of sheet floorings in bathrooms by taking material up on to bath panels and skirtings so that water cannot seep behind them.

First, pin slim triangular beading (25mm square) into the floor/panel angle to support the fold when the flooring is laid. Trim the flooring as before, leaving enough material to lap up the panel/skirting to the desired height. It should reach to just under the lip of the bath, or the top edge of the skirting. Mark and cut as necessary, then apply double-sided tape or bands of adhesive to the surfaces and press into place. Use adhesive to waterproof corner joins.

Neaten skirting upstands by pinning slim beading to the top of the skirting board or to the wall above it to cover the edges.

# LAYING WOODSTRIP FLOORING

If you like the warmth of a natural timber floor finish, laying hardwood strip flooring is the perfect answer.

Most homes have timber floors, formed by nailing flat planks over the supporting joists. From Victorian times until around the time of the Second World War, when timber supplies became scarce, both downstairs and upstairs floors were usually constructed in this way. Nowadays, ground floors are invariably of solid concrete, while floors on upper storeys now usually have chipboard sheets instead of individual floorboards. Since the revival of interest in wood in the Seventies, it has become fashionable to have 'bare boards' as a floor surface.

One way of achieving this is to sand and seal existing floorboards (see Renovating Wood Floors, page 83), provided they are in reasonable condition. If they are not, or you have solid or chipboard floors, you will have to lay a new finish of hardwood timber – known as woodstrip flooring.

## TYPES OF WOODSTRIP

Woodstrip flooring is available in two main types: as solid planks, and as laminated strips (rather like plywood) with a decorative surface veneer. Lengths vary, from as little as 400mm up to 1800mm, and widths range from 70mm up to around 200mm. Thicknesses of either type range between 12 and 23mm.

Both types are usually made up from strips of wood which are shorter and narrower than the finished panel. However, veneered types may be manufactured to resemble one continuous plank, or a basketweave effect.

Both types are generally tongued-and-grooved on their long and their short edges for easy fitting. Some are designed to be fixed to a timber sub-floor by secret nailing, while others are loose-laid using ingenious metal clips to hold adjacent strips together. This means they can be lifted easily if access is needed to underfloor services (nailed-down types can be a problem in this respect). A third method of fixing used by some manufacturers is to apply adhesive along the top of the tongue. Consult the manufacturer's instructions.

A wide range of timber varieties is available in each type, including elm, oak, ash, beech, maple, mahogany and more exotic tropical hardwoods such as iroko and merbau. Laminated types are generally pre-finished; solid types may also be, but some need sealing once they have been laid.

You can lay woodstrip flooring on either timber or solid floors, provided you devote a little time to floor preparation first. If you don't, your expensive new floor surface will soon begin to wear unevenly. One particularly important point concerns the provision of an expansion gap at the edge of the floor, to allow the boards to move slightly as temperature and humidity levels change. If you don't provide this the whole floor may buckle.

### Looking at wood
*From left to right, samples of solid woodstrip flooring, sections of veneered panels, samples of solid wood flooring made up from two strips of wood and a single panel of a different system of veneered flooring.*

## TIMBER SUB-FLOORS

If you plan to lay your new woodstrip flooring over existing floorboards, the first step is to lift the old floorcovering and remove any fixing tacks, staples and the like. Then go over the entire floor surface, punching in the board fixing nails to a depth of 2-3mm with your hammer and nail punch. Use extra flooring nails to secure loose boards, and screw down the ends of any that have warped and are standing proud.

If the surface is very uneven, lay hardboard to disguise the lumps and bumps. Brush water on to the mesh backs of the sheets and stack them back to back in the room for 24 hours. Then pin them down, rough side up, at intervals of about 150mm along the edges and 300mm across the centres. The boards will tighten as they dry out.

Chipboard floors provide a perfect base for woodstrip flooring, so long as the boards are firmly fixed. Use screws to secure any that squeak when you tread on them, especially across the board centres; many builders only secure the sheets at the edges.

## SOLID SUB-FLOORS

Solid concrete sub-floors generally need little preparation unless lifting existing floorcoverings has left lumps of old adhesive all over the place, or the floor itself is decidedly uneven. In either case the simplest remedy is to cover it with a layer of self-smoothing compound, a dense plaster-like material which you mix with water and trowel out on to the floor surface and leave to harden. It raises the floor level by only a few millimetres, and leaves a smooth surface ready for the new covering.

Solid (direct-to-earth) floors in older houses may have no damp course, or the damp-proofing may be defective. If you suspect this, it's essential to treat the floor surface with a damp-proofing sealer first, since otherwise rot can develop in the new floorcovering.

## ADJUSTING THE WOODWORK

You will achieve the neatest finish to your new floor if you prise off the skirting boards all round the room, and replace them once the flooring has been laid. This will then conceal the 10mm expansion gap round the perimeter of the room. You should also trim the feet of door architraves to allow the flooring to fit beneath them. However, if this is impractical you can leave your expansion gap between the new flooring and the face of the skirting instead, and either insert narrow strips of cork to fill the gap or conceal it with quadrant beading pinned to the skirting.

Don't forget that your new flooring will raise the existing floor level noticeably, so take doors which open over it off their hinges *before* you lay the new floor; otherwise, you could be trapped in the room behind an unopenable door. Shorten the door before re-hanging it by carefully planing the lower edge.

## LAYING WOODSTRIP FLOORING

All the hard work involved in putting down woodstrip flooring lies in the preparation; the actual laying, like so many decorating jobs, is simple and proceeds gratifyingly quickly.

**1** *Estimate quantities*
Once you have decided which brand and type of flooring you want to lay, make a note of the plank size so you can estimate accurately how much to buy. As with all flooring, it's best to draw a scale plan of the room first, and decide which way the planks will run. Then measure up accurately to work out the total plank length required. Remember to use the 'face size' – the width of plank that's exposed once the tongues and grooves are assembled – rather than the nominal size. Allow an extra 5 per cent to cope with wastage during cutting and fitting.

### CHECK YOUR NEEDS
- ☐ Solid or laminated floorcovering
- ☐ Hardboard plus fixing pins for uneven timber floors
- ☐ Floorboard nails or wood screws plus bradawl and screwdriver (for fixing loose boards)
- ☐ Self-smoothing compound (for uneven solid floors)
- ☐ Underlay (if recommended by flooring manufacturer)
- ☐ Retractable steel tape measure
- ☐ Claw hammer
- ☐ Tenon saw or electric jig saw
- ☐ Portable workbench
- ☐ Try square
- ☐ Nail punch
- ☐ Craft knife
- ☐ Adjustable template (optional)
- ☐ Woodworking adhesive or fixing pins (as recommended)

**2** *Prepare the wood strips*
Always unpack the strips and leave them in the room where they will be laid for about a week to acclimatize to the temperature and humidity levels in your home. This will help to prevent undue buckling or shrinkage when they are finally laid.

**3** *Fit underlay*
If the manufacturer recommends the use of a special underlay (which may be polythene sheeting, glass fibre matting, or foam), put this down next, and tape or staple the joins together so they don't ruck up as you work.

**4** *Position the first row* ▷
Aim to begin laying alongside a straight, uninterrupted wall if possible; otherwise choose the one with the fewest obstructions. Offer up the first plank to the wall, with 10mm thick offcuts of wood to act as spacers positioned between the wall and the board edge to form the expansion gap. If there are obstacles along the wall, scribe and cut the planks in this first row to fit round them, using your tenon saw or jig saw.

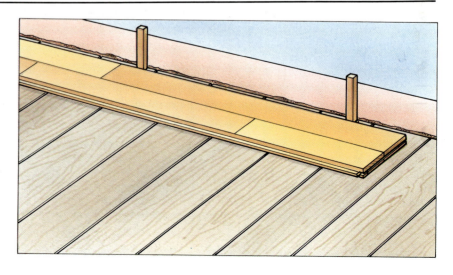

**5** *Fix the first row* ▷
Make sure the grooved edge faces the wall. If the flooring you are using is fixed by secret nailing, drive fixing pins down through the tongues into the sub-floor, punching the heads into the angle, but taking care not to over-drive them or the tongue will split and the other edge of the plank begin to lift. They should be spaced about 300mm apart.

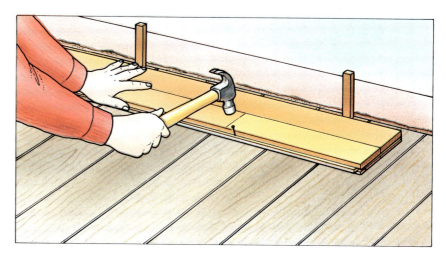

**6** *Using fixing clips* ◁
If you are using fixing clips, the method of fixing will depend on the system. With the type shown here, you just tap the clips into the grooves in the underside of the first board at the recommended intervals, and lay the grooved edge of the board in place against the spacers. When you come to fit subsequent strips, it's important to make sure you stagger the positions of the fixing clips.

**7** *Butting ends of planks* ▷
Lay further planks end to end to complete the first row. Fit them dry first, and trim the end plank so it falls 10mm short from the wall. Most systems recommend using PVA woodworking adhesive to bond the end-to-end butt joints together; apply a little adhesive to one end of each plank and tap it into position, wiping away any surplus adhesive with a damp cloth.

**8** *Lay subsequent rows* ◁
Lay the second (and subsequent) rows of planks by offering their grooved edges up to the tongues of the previous row, and use an offcut over their tongued edges to protect them while you tap the joints tightly closed. With secret nailing, pin through the tongues as before; some types recommend gluing the tongued-and-grooved joint too, so apply a little adhesive along the groove before tapping the plank into place. If you are using the clip system, fit the next row of clips and offer the grooved edge up to the tongue of the first row. Tapping the planks will enable the clips to engage and lock the boards together.

**9** *Arranging the joins*
Take care to stagger the butt joins in adjacent rows as you proceed across the floor for an attractive finish; you can always start a row with an offcut to achieve this effect.

**10** *Awkward shapes* ▷
Where planks run up to awkwardly-shaped obstacles such as door architraves or central heating pipes, either scribe the end of the plank to fit or use an adjustable template to transfer the outline of the obstacle on to it, ready for cutting. You may need a coping saw to make intricate cut-outs.

**11** *The last row of planks* ▷
The last row of planks will probably have to be cut down in width to allow them to be fitted. After laying the last whole row, position the next plank on top of it and use another plank (or an offcut) to scribe the plank which is to be cut to fit in place, allowing for the expansion gap. Then cut the planks down to the required width with your saw. With secret nailing, the last row of planks will have lost their tongued edges. For glued systems, the adhesive will hold the last row in place, but if you have just been nailing the tongues you will have to fix the last row with pins driven through the plank faces. Punch the pins in with your nail punch, and fill the holes with wood filler.

With clips, it may be impossible to slip the last strip into place with the clips fitted. Here it's best simply to glue the final tongued-and-grooved joint for a neat finish.

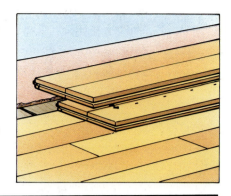

**12** *Expansion gaps* ▷
Finish off by removing the spacers all round the room and replacing the skirting boards so they cover the expansion gap (see page 30).

If you left the skirtings in place, cut and fit special cork strips (supplied by the flooring manufacturer) to fill the gap all round the perimeter, or pin quadrant beading to the skirting to cover the gap. Add a tapered timber fillet across the door threshold (see page 81).

**13** *Polish or varnish*
Sweep up sawdust and clear the room, ready for the floor to receive its final polish. If you have to varnish unsealed planks, vacuum-clean the floor thoroughly and then apply three coats of varnish in the same way as for a stripped floor (see pages 83–86).

▽ *Perfectly floored*
Beautifully laid woodstrip flooring makes a hard wearing, attractive surface which is easy on the feet. Here it has been used in a kitchen, but it is equally suitable for any room in the house. There are different grades, suitable for various amounts of wear.

## BRIGHT IDEA

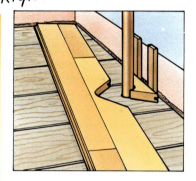

**Pipework** One of the trickiest obstacles to deal with when laying floors of this type is central heating and hot water pipes. Measure the distance of the pipe from the wall and drill a hole in the flooring to correspond with this, slightly larger than the diameter of the pipe. Don't forget to allow for the expansion gap at the edge of the board behind the pipe. Then use an electric jig saw to cut diagonally outwards from the hole, towards the edge of the board. Fit the offcut of board behind the pipe as shown, not forgetting to allow for the expansion gap. Apply woodworking adhesive to the cut surface, then position the main part of the board as usual. Any unsightly gaps can be filled with offcuts of cork, or sawdust mixed to a paste with PVA woodworking adhesive.

# MOSAIC AND WOOD SHEET FLOORING

If you like the look of wood floors, you can choose easy-to-lay mosaic tiles or use plywood or chipboard for economy.

Wood has made a big comeback in the floorcovering stakes over the last ten years or so. It makes a practical, warm, comfortable finish for floors in any room in the house, and is not hard on the feet in rooms like the kitchen where you are standing a lot of the time. People who are lucky enough to have wooden floorboards which are in reasonable condition may have sanded, sealed and polished them for a fashionable stripped pine look. An effective, although more expensive alternative is to lay a decorative hardwood strip flooring.

However, these aren't the only options if you like the feel and look of wood floors, but can't afford hardwood planks, or your floorboards are too scruffy to expose to public gaze.

### WOOD MOSAIC FLOOR TILES

One option is to lay mosaic floor tiles, which are square tiles made up from a number of small fingers of hardwood.

The fingers themselves may be solid wood or veneer on a cheaper softwood backing, and are usually arranged in a basketweave pattern; however, other arrangements are also available. The fingers are usually about 15-20mm wide and 150mm long. There is a wide range of wood types used, including oak, mahogany, teak, iroko and merbau. Some tiles are supplied sealed, others have to be varnished to seal them once they have been laid.

The fingers may be mounted on a felt backing sheet which acts as an underlay, helping to cushion sound as well as bonding the fingers together; the result is a sheet that will bend along the joint lines. Alternatively, the fingers may be wired or stuck together to produce a rigid tile. In either case, tiles are generally either 300mm or 450mm square.

*Basketweave effect*
*Wood mosaic floor tiles in a basketweave pattern create a warm, relatively hardwearing finish, without great expense. They look equally good in a modern or traditional setting.*

## MAN-MADE BOARDS

Another alternative is to use one of the man-made board materials – hardboard, chipboard or plywood – to form a new surface, either laid on top of the existing floor or, if you have suspended timber floors and the board is strong enough, in place of the old floorboards. The only drawback is that these sheet materials make it difficult to get at under-floor pipes and cables.

**Hardboard** is the cheapest material you can use, and is more generally found as an underlay put down to form a smooth surface beneath tile and sheet floor-coverings (including carpet). It should be used only over existing timber floors, fixed with hardboard pins. The surface can be varnished, stained, or painted to give an attractive and economical (if not very durable) floor finish. The boards themselves come in standard 2440 × 1220mm sheets, 3mm thick.

**Chipboard** has actually taken the place of traditional floorboards as the usual decking material for suspended floors in modern homes, and is intended to be covered over with a decorative floor-covering. However, its oatmealy surface texture resembles a cork floor when varnished. Ordinary chipboard can be used on top of existing timber or solid floors, but if it will replace existing floorboards the stronger, denser flooring grade of board must be used instead. Boards measure a standard 2440 × 1220mm, with flooring-grade boards also available in 2440 × 610mm sizes. The latter are often tongued and grooved, which ensures draught- and dust-free joints on suspended floors.

**Plywood** is the third option. Because the surface veneers are good-quality timber, stain or varnish can give an attractive finish even with the blandest birch-faced boards. Boards faced with teak, oak, sapele, or mahogany veneers can look quite stunning and very expensive. Again, the boards come in a standard 2440 × 1220mm size, but they are also available in smaller sheets (down to 610mm square), which may be more convenient to use and can create some unusual effects. Choose the 6 or 10mm thickness to cover existing floors; the thicker grades are comparatively pricey.

## PAINTED FINISHES

As an alternative to stain and varnish, all three board types can be given a painted finish – either plain, or one of the many popular wall effects such as marbling or graining, even stencilling. To protect the paintwork, apply at least three coats of clear polyurethane varnish, allowing each to dry thoroughly and rubbing down lightly between coats, see page 86.

---

### CHECK YOUR NEEDS
**For laying mosaic tiles:**
- ☐ Mosaic floor tiles
- ☐ Flooring adhesive
- ☐ Brush or spreader for adhesive
- ☐ String and chalk
- ☐ Retractable steel tape measure
- ☐ Pencil and craft knife
- ☐ Tenon saw or power jig saw
- ☐ Portable workbench

- ☐ Glasspaper and sanding block *or* power sander
- ☐ Varnish (for unsealed types)
- ☐ Lint-free cloth and brush
- ☐ Cork expansion strips *or* quadrant beading

**For laying sheet materials:**
- ☐ Hardboard, chipboard or plywood
- ☐ Retractable steel tape measure
- ☐ Pencil, straight edge and craft knife
- ☐ Panel saw *or* power jig saw
- ☐ Portable workbench
- ☐ Hardboard pins and pin hammer (for fixing hardboard and plywood)
- ☐ Woodscrews plus power drill and bits and screwdriver (for fixing chipboard)
- ☐ Stain or varnish, plus brushes

---

## LAYING MOSAIC FLOOR TILES

The job of laying mosaic floor tiles is a comparatively straightforward one, similar to any other floor-tiling project in terms of preparation and setting-out.

**1** *Calculate quantities*
Start by finding out the size of the floor tiles you intend to lay; most are either 300mm or 450mm square. Then draw a scale plan of the room so you can work out how many rows of tiles will be needed to cover the floor area, and how many tiles will be needed in each row. Multiply the two figures together and add five per cent extra to allow for wastage. Estimate the numbers needed to fill awkward areas such as bay windows by counting each cut tile as a whole tile.

**2** *Prepare the floor*
Prepare the sub-floor as already described in Laying Woodstrip Flooring (pages 75–78). Briefly, this involves punching in nail heads and securing loose boards on timber floors (plus laying a hardboard overlay if the boards are very uneven, see page 82), and putting down a self-smoothing compound over uneven solid ones. Decide whether to remove and refix the skirtings, or work with them in place, and shave the door bottoms so they will clear the new raised floor level.

**3** *Temper the tiles*
Store the mosaic panels unpacked in the room where they will be laid for at least seven days, to allow them to acclimatize to temperature and humidity. This will help minimize shrinkage and other problems when the tiles are laid.

**4** *Start in the centre ▷*
Find your starting point in the centre of the room, in exactly the same way as for laying cork and vinyl floor tiles (see pages 67–70 for full details). It's best to work in this way to ensure an even border of cut tiles at the perimeter of the room, although any variations will not be so noticeable here as they would be with patterned vinyl tiles. If you are confident that the room is square, you could start laying in one corner instead, but it's difficult to guarantee a perfect result.

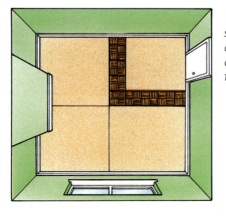

**5** *Spread the adhesive*
When you are happy with the setting-out, spread some adhesive in the quarter of the room farthest from the door. The adhesive usually comes in a tub with its own spreader.

**6** *Stick down the tiles* ▷
Lay the first tile to your guidelines. Press it down firmly with your hands, and then tap all over it with a hammer to ensure a really good bond, using an offcut of wood to protect the tile surface. Then lay further whole tiles out from the centre point towards the perimeter of the room, filling each quarter of the floor area in turn. Make sure that tile edges butt up tightly and align squarely with each other; slight errors can accumulate into big ones at the end of a row.

If you get any adhesive on the face of the tiles, wipe it off with a damp cloth immediately. If it starts to dry, remove it with wire wool and white spirit.

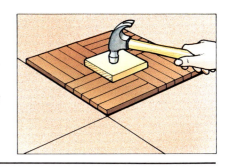

**7** *Fill in round edges* ◁
When you have laid all the whole tiles, start filling in the cut pieces at the perimeter and round obstacles. For straight edge strips, simply use a tile or offcut to scribe the tile to be cut (positioned on top of the last whole tile). Place a scrap of wood 10mm wide against the wall to allow for the essential expansion gap. Cut the tile down to the required size, and bed it in place. Where you have to cut tiles round awkward shapes such as door architraves and central heating pipes, either scribe the panels directly or use an adjustable template device to transcribe the outline of the obstacle and use a coping saw to make cut-outs.

**8** *Neaten round edges* ▷
Replace the skirtings; if you left them in place, either fit cork expansion strips into the 10mm expansion gap or cover it with quadrant beading pinned to the lower face of the skirting board to cover it. It's best to decorate the beading to match the skirting boards before fixing it in place; you can touch up the pin holes afterwards.

**9** *Finish the threshold* ▷
Fit an angled timber fillet at the door threshold. There are various types available, including some with male or female tongues or grooves to fit hardwood floors. For most floors, however, the simple profile shown at the bottom on the right is the best choice.

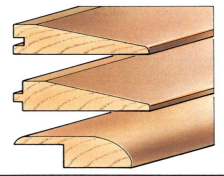

**10** *Clean and seal*
Sweep up dust and debris, and polish sealed types. With unsealed types, lightly sand and vacuum-clean the floor and then use a tack rag (a clean cloth soaked in white spirit) to ensure you have a clean surface. Then apply three coats of sealer (see pages 83–86 for more details).

### LAYING SHEET MATERIALS

The one awkward point about laying sheet materials such as hardboard, chipboard and plywood is the sheer size of the boards. It's a good idea to decide early on whether it would be easier to work with smaller panels – 1220mm squares, for example, or even 610mm squares. Then you can get your supplier to cut the larger boards down for you, for laying. It's essential that boards are machined, so as to make true squares.

**1** *Prepare timber floors*
You are most likely to be laying sheet materials over an existing timber floor surface, so start by punching in raised nail heads and securing loose boards. Remove skirtings if necessary.

**2** *Plan the layout* ▷
Dry-lay the sheets on the floor to check the best fit. If the flooring is to be on show, position the central boards first, aligning them with focal points in the room such as a fireplace or bay window. Alternatively, you may want to start along the length of a fitting, such as a row of kitchen units. Try to stagger the joins between boards in adjacent rows. Lay only the whole sheets at this stage.

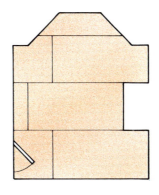

**3** *Lay the first sheet*
When you have found the best layout, clear the sheets which are to be cut to one side. Leave the sheet you are going to lay first in place, and move the other whole sheets to the side of the room.

**4 Nailing hardboard and plywood ▷**
With hardboard and plywood, fix the sheets with hardboard pins (diamond-headed pins) or panel pins driven in at 150mm intervals along the board edges and at 300mm intervals across the boards. Punch in the pin heads and cover with wood stopper.

**5 Screwing down chipboard ▽**
With chipboard, drill pilot holes at 300mm intervals along the board edges, and at 600mm intervals across the board centre. Countersink the holes, then drive in the fixing screws (No 8, 30mm) and fill the holes.

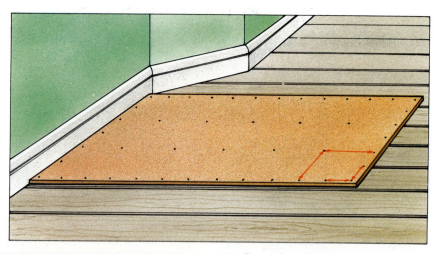

**6 Fit smaller pieces**
With all the whole sheets laid, cut and fit the perimeter strips, leaving a 10mm expansion gap as before. Cover this with the skirting board (if you removed it) or with quadrant beading.

**7 Finish the surface**
Fill any unsightly gaps with wood filler to match the final floor colour. Sand the board surface lightly, sweep up dust and then stain or varnish the board. Alternatively, use one of the many decorative effects – such as marbling or graining.

## BRIGHT IDEA

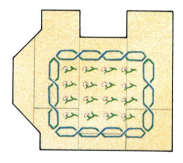

**Carpet style** A painted hardboard floor is one of the most economical finishes. You can create a richer illusion by painting it, then stencilling a border to imitate a carpet square in the middle of the room. Apply a primer/undercoat (you may need two coats if the hardboard is a dark colour), then use oil-based paints for the decoration. Protect with three coats of clear varnish.

**◁ High gloss finish**
Panels of plywood, 610mm square, have been laid with the grain running in alternating directions in this modern living room. The rich colours of the wood are brought out, and the surface protected, by applying several coats of varnish.

# RENOVATING WOOD FLOORS

A natural timber floor can look beautiful if it's sanded, sealed and polished... and it's cheaper than laying carpet.

Timber floors which have been covered with carpet or lino for years, or have varnish or paint which is wearing thin, can be renovated and given a long lasting protective finish. First identify the type of floor you have.

**Softwood floorboards** You may have plain, softwood floorboards – either square-edged or tongued-and-grooved planks up to 25mm thick and 150 to 230mm wide, nailed to the floor joists.

**Hardwood flooring** Another type is a decorative hardwood floor. This is in fact a floorcovering laid over the structural floor surface (timber or concrete). Oak, mahogany and teak are the most commonly-found woods, although other more exotic types are also used.

There are several kinds of hardwood floor. The first consists of slim hardwood planks that are either nailed to the floorboards beneath or are held in place by a system of metal clips. Cheaper versions use veneered plywood strips instead of solid timber.

The second type is hardwood block flooring, often referred to as parquet. This consists of small blocks of wood up to 230mm long and 75mm wide which are usually laid in a herringbone or basketweave pattern. Older or more expensive types are blocks up to 25mm thick, bedded in a bitumen adhesive. Cheaper imitations are again veneered.

The third type is the mosaic panel – a floor tile made up by gluing small fingers of wood on a backing sheet to make up a panel 300 or 450mm (12 or 18in) square. These are laid like any floor tile, either on an adhesive bed or loose on top of a special underlay.

**Deciding on the treatment** The usual treatment involves sanding the floor with a powered sanding machine to remove the old finish and expose clean, fresh wood ready for sealing and polishing. Any solid wood floor can easily tolerate this, but if the surface is only a veneer then power sanding with a coarse abrasive could go right through it. In this case, gentler methods such as a hand-held belt or orbital sander are advisable.

## BEFORE YOU START

Check the floor structure for signs of woodworm or rot. If you find woodworm, tackle it by lifting the floorboards and spraying water-based woodworm fluid over the affected surfaces before re-laying the boards. If you find rot, call in an expert to assess the problem; DIY treatment is often possible, but may not be effective if dry rot is present.

If the floorboards need lifting during preparation (see pages 84–85) you could put in underfloor insulation. This can be done by stapling plastic netting between the joists to support glass fibre loft insulation, or by resting strips of rigid polystyrene insulation on nails driven into the sides of the joists. With suspended timber ground floors, make sure that air bricks are clear so the underfloor void is well ventilated, or rot can get a hold.

## TOOLS AND EQUIPMENT

The only specialist tools you'll need for this job are two powered sanding machines, which you can hire. The larger machine is called a drum or floor sander; it resembles a cylinder lawnmower and drives belts of abrasive round a large drum. It has a built-in sawdust extraction unit. The smaller machine is needed for sanding the parts the larger one cannot reach; you may be offered a belt or a disc type. The former is better because it will not leave scratch marks across the grain.

When you take delivery of the machines, make sure that you are shown exactly how to operate them, and get plenty of abrasive sheets and belts in coarse, medium and fine grades. Buy or hire a face mask at the same time, so you don't choke on the sawdust. Safety goggles and ear defenders are also a good idea, though not essential.

*Down to wood*
*A sanded and sealed softwood floor is an economical and attractive finish. It is easy to maintain and helps to give any room a spacious, airy feeling.*

## CHECK YOUR NEEDS

- ☐ Overalls and gloves
- ☐ Face mask with spare filters
- ☐ Goggles/ear defenders (optional)
- ☐ Masking tape (for sealing doors)
- ☐ Claw hammer
- ☐ Nail punch
- ☐ Flooring nails (for softwood)
- ☐ Flooring adhesive (for hardwood)
- ☐ Padsaw or jigsaw (for tongued-and-grooved floors)
- ☐ Drum and small belt sander
- ☐ Coarse, medium and fine abrasives (on sale or return)
- ☐ Glasspaper and sanding block
- ☐ Wood filler and wood dye
- ☐ Wood bleach (for deep stains)
- ☐ Vacuum cleaner
- ☐ White spirit and clean rags
- ☐ Varnish (5 litres will be needed for an average-sized room)
- ☐ 75mm and 25mm paint brushes
- ☐ Floor polish and polisher

### SAFE SANDING ▷

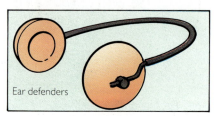
Ear defenders

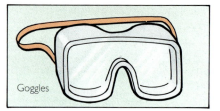
Goggles

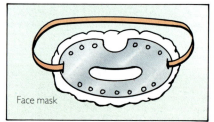
Face mask

☐ When using a floor sander, always wear a face mask so you don't inhale the clouds of fine dust which always seem to escape the machine's dust bag. Wear goggles and ear defenders.

☐ Seal the door with masking tape to keep dust out of the rest of the house, and open windows for ventilation.

☐ Don't wear loose clothing; close-fitting overalls are best. Protect your hands with gloves when handling the abrasive sheets and belts. Always unplug the machine when changing them.

☐ Keep the sander's flex out of harm's way by draping it over your shoulder.

☐ Never start the machine with the drum in contact with the floor, or it will snatch away from you uncontrollably. Stop it immediately if the abrasive tears, or you may jam the drum.

☐ Lastly, don't let children touch the machines under any circumstances.

### PREPARING SOFTWOOD FLOORS

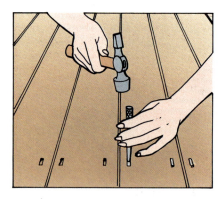

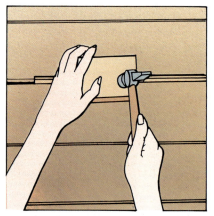

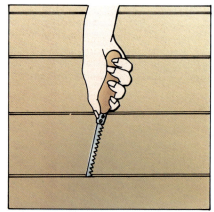

**1** *Getting a good surface △*
With softwood floors, using a nail punch and hammer, check that all nail heads are punched at least 3mm below the surface. Remove any tacks which have been used to hold down any previous flooring. Fix any loose boards by driving in cut flooring nails close to existing nail positions, to minimize the risk of piercing hidden pipes or cables. Use deeply-countersunk screws if warped boards keep pulling the nails up.

**2** *Filling large gaps △*
If there are substantial gaps between boards, fill them with slim strips of timber planed to width, glued and hammered into place. Gaps everywhere suggest that it would be far quicker to lift all the boards, to re-lay them so they butt together tightly, and to add one or two new boards as necessary to make up the gap when all the old boards have been replaced. Check the measurements of your floorboards before buying new ones: there is a range of standard sizes, but if you have old or unusual boards, you may need to order planks cut to size.

**3** *Replacing rotten boards △*
If you find boards that are split or otherwise badly damaged, replace them with new boards. To lift tongued-and-grooved boards, first cut through the tongues along each edge with a padsaw (a long slim saw which looks rather like a knife) or a powered jigsaw. Beware of electric cables and pipes running under the boards. Then prize the board up from one end with a crowbar or similar lever, using a scrap of timber to protect the end of the adjacent sound board. Cut the new board to fit and nail it in place. If it's not as thick as the others, add cardboard packing under it.

**4** *Turning the boards* △
If the surface is badly damaged, for example through repeated layers of lino being tacked down or badly stained, you can try turning the floorboards. The undersides will be marked where they cross the joists, but apart from that they should be in better condition (woodworm and rot permitting) than the top surface. Lift just one or two boards first to check their condition.

**5** *Cleaning up* △
Finally, sweep the floor. Then make sure you've got all your tools and equipment with you, close the door to the rest of the house and seal round it with masking tape to stop dust from spreading everywhere. Open the room windows for ventilation, and to help the dust clear as you work.

### PREPARING HARDWOOD FLOORS

With hardwood floors, check for loose blocks or panels, and stick down any that you find with flooring adhesive. Hardwood flooring is often secret nailed in place, particularly the narrow plank types and some of the mosaics. If sections have worked loose they should be re-fixed in the same way, by secret nailing through the tongue into the joist. Watch out for electrical installations.

### SANDING FLOORBOARDS

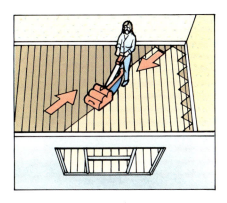
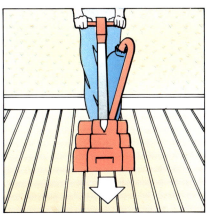

**1** *Starting to sand* △
Fit a coarse abrasive sheet to the sander, plug in and switch on to test that it's working. Then start sanding with the machine in one corner of the room. The aim is to work diagonally to begin with, to ensure that all the boards are sanded level with one another, so start by heading for the opposite corner of the room. Then turn round and run back over the same strip. Continue sanding the whole floor diagonally in this way, taking care not to damage skirtings as you reach the end of each run. Replace abrasive sheets as they become worn.

**2** *Getting a good finish* △
Next, change to medium-grade abrasive and sand the floor parallel with the board direction, again going over each strip in both directions. Work as close to the skirting boards as you can without scoring them with the side of the machine. Then switch to fine abrasive and repeat the whole process again. Empty the dust bag regularly into heavy-duty plastic refuse sacks. It's also a good idea to vacuum the floor from time to time to cut down on the amount of fine dust flying around. Also change the filter in your face mask regularly so it doesn't get clogged up.

**3** *Down to details* △
You can now tackle the edges, and any other parts that the drum sander couldn't reach, using the belt or orbital sander. Work through coarse, medium and fine grades. Finish off by hand-sanding any bits that have been missed.

**4** *Cleaning up*
When you've finished sanding, sweep and vacuum-clean thoroughly to remove as much dust as possible. Pay particular attention to joints between the boards, and to the corners. Then use a tack rag – a clean cloth soaked in white spirit – to wipe over the boards.

### BRIGHT IDEA

**Keep it cool** If you don't like the yellowing effect of varnish, experiment with one of these techniques. Bleach the wood first with a proprietary wood bleach or a mixture of oxalic acid and methylated spirit. Alternatively, prime the boards with a 50/50 solution of white emulsion paint and water, rubbing it into the grain.

Any water-based solution will raise the grain slightly, so apply this before the final sanding. You can also add 10 per cent white eggshell paint to 90 per cent varnish.

## SANDING HARDWOOD FLOORS

A floor of hardwood timber planks does not usually require quite such drastic treatment as a softwood floor. You should find that simply sanding up and down the planks with first medium and then fine abrasive is sufficient to remove the existing finish and any slight irregularities. Don't forget to check that the floor is not veneered – you may have to lift a splinter of wood from a corner of the room with a penknife.

A hardwood block floor should also be fairly easy to tackle. The main problem is deciding in which direction to sand the floor. You should avoid sanding across the grain of the wood. So a herringbone pattern should be sanded up and down the room, while a basketweave pattern should be sanded diagonally. You will then have sanded the grain of the wood diagonally (as close as you can get to sanding with the grain, which gives the best finish). Depending on the condition of the floor, only medium and fine abrasives should be necessary.

Any hardwood block borders round the edge of the room should be sanded with a belt or orbital sander.

## SEALING THE FLOOR

**1 Filling holes** △
With clean, fresh wood exposed, now is the time to fill nail and screw holes, plus any other gaps between the floorboards which have not been filled with wood strips. Use wood filler, adding wood dye to the filler if necessary to match the shade of the wood more accurately. Use wood bleach on any deep stains that have not been removed by the sanding. When the filler is hard, sand down locally and wipe up dust with a tack rag as before.

**2 Adding colour** △
You can change the colour of the floor if you wish by using wood dyes. Follow the manufacturer's instructions carefully; in most cases a single coat of dye is wiped on to the floor with a lint-free cloth, working along the grain.

Test the effect of the dye on an offcut first, working over a large area to develop the technique. The porosity of wood varies, so test the dye on new wood to see that it matches. Also check the finished effect by varnishing the test pieces. After you have done the whole floor, wipe with a clean dry cloth to remove surplus dye.

**3 Apply varnish** △
Thin the first coat of varnish with about 10 per cent white spirit on softwood; use it straight from the tin on hardwood. If the wood is porous, it may be quicker to wipe the first coat on with a cloth, rather than using a brush. Allow it to dry for as long as the manufacturer recommends; then sand the surface lightly with fine abrasive on a sanding block, and wipe over with a tack rag to remove the dust. Apply two further coats using a 75mm brush, cutting in at the edges with a smaller one. Sand as before. Always work back towards the door so you can get out easily.

**4 Using coloured varnish**
You can also apply coloured varnishes. For an even finish, it is best to prime the boards with clear varnish first, as above, before building up two or three coats of coloured varnish. A final protective coat of clear varnish can be added for extra protection.

**5 Polishing it up**
Finish the job by polishing the floor surface – either by hand or using a hired floor polisher. Make sure that any rugs or carpets laid over the floor have non-slip pads on their undersides.

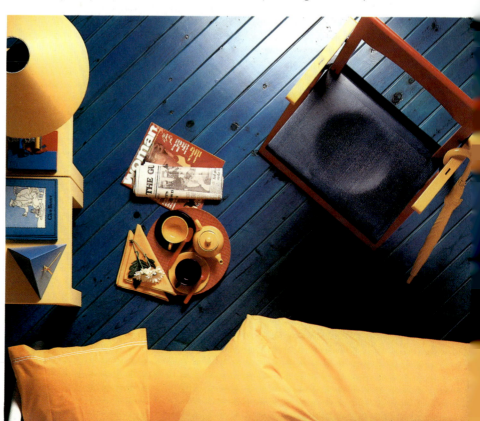

**Colour it rich** ▷
Tinted varnish adds a depth of colour to the floor. Here, tongued-and-grooved boards have been varnished in a strong blue, to contrast with the yellow furnishings.

# LOOKING AFTER THE OUTSIDE

A smart, well maintained exterior keeps your home weatherproof and increases its value.

The outside of your home faces daily damage from the weather. An annual check helps to keep it in good repair, and avoids the problems of penetrating damp, rotting window frames and a leaking roof. If problems are spotted early, expensive work can be avoided.

As well as preventing rot and other damage, exterior decoration can add to the value and appearance of your home – but only if you choose carefully. Window frames, doors and exterior paintwork must be in sympathy with the style and character of the house. A house which looks radically different from others in the street, painted in a garish colour (or worse still, covered in artificial stone cladding), with windows and doors which do not match the architectural stye of the original building may prove difficult to sell.

## KEEPING THE STYLE

When replacing parts of the house, such as bricks, tiles, doors, windows and chimney pots, try to match the original. Many modern materials, although excellent in themselves, may be out of keeping with a Victorian house or one built in the 1920s or 30s. Before you start work, visit architectural salvage yards and look at suppliers' catalogues and leaflets.

## UP ON THE ROOF

The roof is the most important part of the exterior of your home. Leaks can cause interior damp, mould and fungus. When checking the roof, stand outside your home and study the slates or tiles and the chimney through binoculars. If it is not possible to see the roof, ask a professional roofer to check for you.

**Chimneys** Check that the chimney stacks are straight, not leaning over to one side. Look for cracks down the brickwork. If you find either of these problems, seek professional advice. Check whether the mortar joints between the bricks on the chimney stack are in good condition. Look at the mortar flaunching around the pots. The purpose of flaunching is to prevent rain water getting into the chimney stack. If it

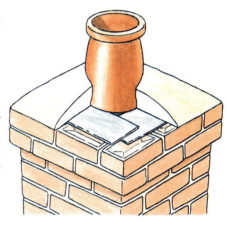

△ *Check your chimney*
Check the flaunching around the base of chimneys. It should be free from cracks.

▽ *Fault finding*
Check the points shown here at least once a year to keep your home wind and weatherproof.

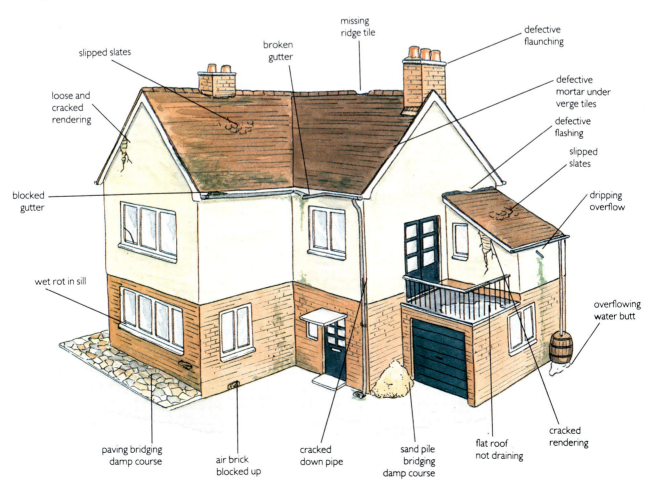

is cracked, then it must be replaced.

Chimney pots can be bought new or secondhand. Replacement is best left to a builder. Unused pots can be capped but leave space for ventilation.

**Tiles and slates** Look for damp patches inside the loft. These indicate that there are tiles or slates loose or missing. Tiles usually slip because the nails holding them have corroded away. They can also suffer from a condition called delamination which is caused by water entering the tile or slate, freezing then splitting off the top layer. In both cases, the affected tiles or slates should be replaced by a roofing expert. If the problem is widespread, a new roof is needed.

**Ridge tiles** Check the ridge tiles and the mortar under the tiles or slates at the edge of the roof. Re-fix loose tiles or cracked mortar.

**Flat roofs** Check that the covering is free from splits, cracks or blisters. Flat roofs need annual treatment with bitumen or a similar waterproofing compound designed for use on roofs to keep them in good condition.

**Flashing** Check the flashing around chimney stacks and between flat roofs and the walls of the house. If it is faulty, there will be damp patches inside the house. DIY flashing is inexpensive and easy to apply.

△ *Replacing flashing*
*Replacement flashing can be bought in easy-to-apply rolls.*

## RAINWATER GOODS
Damaged or blocked rainwater goods (the name for gutters and downpipes) can result in internal damp.

**Blockages** Once or twice a year check that gutters are free from leaves, old bird's nests etc (don't remove new nests, it is unkind and unnecessary as the birds will be there only for a few weeks). Check for splits or sags in the guttering by running water through them via a hosepipe.

**Repairs** New lengths of guttering can be used to replace badly damaged sections. Older houses have black iron rainwater goods which are sometimes quite ornate. It would spoil the appearance of the house to replace these with plastic, so visit an architectural salvage yard to find something suitable.

## THE WALLS
Serious faults in walls can include bowing and cracking, both of which need professional attention. More common faults include the failure of mortar joints between bricks and sometimes failure of the bricks themselves.

**Replacing bricks** Individual bricks which are damaged can often be replaced by a matching brick or by removing the brick and turning it round to the undamaged side. If damage is extensive, the answer may be to apply some sort of rendering.

**Repairing mortar** Where mortar joints between bricks are crumbling or missing, they must be replaced. The old mortar must be removed so that there is a sound surface to work on. Use a ready-mixed mortar and make sure that the colour matches the old surrounding joints. The joint should be finished to match the others too. Straight weatherstruck joints look odd if the rest are rounded.

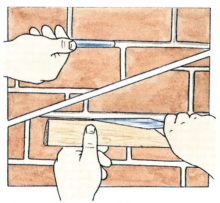

△ *Renewing mortar joints*
*Make sure new mortar joints match those already in place. They can be curved (top), or straight and flat (bottom).*

**Rendering** is the top surface which covers the bricks. It can be painted, or an effect like pebbledash which needs no painting. Rendering can often lose its key and break away from the wall in chunks. While small cracks can be effectively covered by a coat of exterior paint, larger scale damage needs professional attention. If the damage is widespread, all the rendering must be removed and replaced.

**Cladding** Many houses have cladding on the top half of the walls. This can be either tiles or timber. Wall-hung tiles can be replaced in the same way as roof tiles. Most tiles can be colour matched. Timber shiplap or shingles can be replaced with new timber or with one of the new low-maintenance plastic ranges.

**Damp course** When checking walls, look carefully around the base of the house to make sure the damp-proof course is not bridged by garden soil or other material. The damp-proof course has a row of air bricks below it, so it is reasonably easy to spot. These airbricks must never be blocked up as they supply ventilation to suspended timber floors inside the house.

## DOORS AND WINDOWS
Many houses have been built with doors and windows made from untreated softwood – resulting in rot on a grand scale.

**Checking for rot** To check for wet rot, push a pointed tool into the door and window frames at intervals. If you feel resistance, all is well. If the point goes right in, rot is present. Small scale rot can be dealt with using a proprietary wood repair system. These small kits contain filler for the hole left when the affected part has been cut away, and a rot inhibitor. Gaps between the window or door frame and the surrounding wall can be filled with waterproof mastic.

**Replacing doors and windows** Doors and windows in the wrong style can spoil the exterior of your house. There is a very good selection of replacement doors and windows, so finding something in the right style should not be difficult. Choose hardwood doors as they last longer than the softwood type.

Replacement windows are available in a choice of aluminium, uPVC, hardwood or softwood frames and double or single glazed panes. You should take into account the price range, the size of window openings and the age and style of the property and its neighbours. It may well be worth paying the extra to fit double glazed panes if you have to replace a window, but make sure the new window is in style with the house.

## ARTIFICIAL STONE CLADDING
Think twice before applying artificial 'stone' cladding. It can have a disastrous effect on the appearance and the value of your home.
☐ **Value** You may like the cladding, a potential purchaser may not, especially if it spoils interesting features.
☐ **Cladding dangers** There are a number of cowboy operators in the stone cladding business. If not bolted securely to the wall, water can get behind and damage the wall. In frosty weather, the water may freeze and force sections of cladding away, which could be serious if someone is standing below when a block falls off.

# EXTERIOR DECORATING

Proper maintenance of the woodwork and rendering on the outside of your house will protect the fabric as well as keep it looking smart.

Decorating the outside of a house involves very similar techniques to those used inside, with two important differences. First, you will have to work at high levels, and must have suitable and safe equipment to do so. Second, the main objective is not to make the house look better, but to protect it from water penetration, so it is vital to use the right materials, and preparation work is even more important than indoors.

**Plan ahead** Decorating a house is a large task, so plan the job carefully. If you have your own equipment, you can spread the work over many weekends, but if it is hired you may need to spend a week or more of your holidays on it. Don't work in wet, windy or frosty weather, as this will spoil the finish or reduce its life. Follow the sun round the house, so that the surface is dry and you are not working in a glare. Make a shopping list of every item you will need and shop before you start so you don't waste good decorating time.

**Order of work** Get any repair work out of the way before starting preparation. Start at the top, cleaning out the gutters, and work down. Prepare and paint all roof-level woodwork, and gutters if cast-iron. If painting walls, prepare the remaining woodwork and any metalwork next, to avoid messing up the fresh paint. Then do the walls, dividing each one into manageable sections. Continue by painting upstairs windows, any downpipes, then the remaining woodwork.

**Access equipment** As this will only be needed infrequently, hiring may be a better option than buying. Local hire shops can provide everything you need, but book it in advance. The basic item is a ladder: to calculate how high it has to reach, add together the ceiling heights of your home and add one metre. Then add an extra 2-3m to allow you to lean the ladder at a convenient angle. You may also need accessories: ladder stays to hold them away from the wall; bolt-on adjustable legs for use on uneven ground; tool trays and clamps for holding paint cans.

If you have a big house on which large areas of masonry have to be painted, a scaffold tower may make the job much easier as you work standing

*Putting up a good front*
*Maintaining woodwork, rendering and masonry not only gives your home a smart appearance but also protects it from the weather.*

on the platform rather than balancing on the rungs of a ladder.

**Paints for woodwork** Use knotting solution to seal the knots in any new wood and primer on all areas of bare wood (quick-drying acrylic ones speed up the work). Then proceed just as you would indoors, but make sure everything is suitable for exterior use.

If your house is new and the woodwork has been treated with a low-sheen natural timber finish, recoat with a similar product, ideally the same one used by the builders.

If the paintwork is in such bad condition that it has to be completely stripped off, take the opportunity of using one of the new micro-porous or 'breathing' paint systems. These allow moisture to escape from the timber but not to penetrate the paint. This prevents the main cause of paint breakdown – cracking caused by moisture underneath, leading to further water penetration and more cracking.

**Paints for masonry** Previously painted stone, brickwork or rendering is best redecorated with exterior grade emulsion or 'reinforced' emulsion containing mineral or fibre particles. The particles make the finish very long-lasting; but it is more expensive. They also give a rough, matt look, whereas ordinary emulsion is smooth, which may be more desirable on some types of house. Cheaper brands of reinforced emulsion only come in a limited range of popular pastel colours, but some of the more expensive ones are also made in strong traditional colours.

A third possibility is cement paint, which is relatively cheap but comes as a powder which you have to mix yourself. It is not suitable for walls previously finished with smooth emulsion or gloss paint, which do not provide sufficient adhesion.

All these paints are water-based. In most cases two coats are needed.

Oil-based paints suitable for masonry, giving a glossy or satin finish, are obtainable, but they have to be thinned with white spirit.

If you are considering painting brickwork for the first time, think twice: remember that it will just create more maintenance work, as it should be re-painted every five years.

**Paints for metal** Items such as metal windows, gates and gutters should never be decorated with any water-based products as this would set up rust. Use metal primers and oil-based paints, or one of the all-in-one finishing paints designed especially for metals (see Renovating Iron and Steel). Cast-iron gutters should be coated inside with gloss or bitumen paint.

**How much paint?** The quantity of paint required to do the woodwork will obviously depend on how many windows, doors and other timber elements there are.

Don't forget to allow for the barge boards, fascia boards and soffits; also rainwater goods if cast iron; plastic ones don't need painting.

Here is a rough formula for working out how much wall paint to buy. Start by measuring the length of each wall and multiply by the height (about 5.5 metres on an average two-storey house). Ignore doors and windows and allow one litre for every 6.5 sq metres if the surface is smoothly rendered; or 3 sq metres for rough finishes such as pebbledash.

## PAINTING WOODWORK AND METAL

If the paintwork is still reasonably sound, the procedure is exactly the same as for indoor painting: sand down to provide a key for the new paint, then apply an undercoat and topcoat, or two finishing coats. The weather usually takes its toll out of doors, so some repair work may be needed on exposed surfaces.

**2 Make good rotten wood** ▷
Rain penetrating under flaking paint causes wet rot which weakens timber, making it first feel spongy, then disintegrate in patches. If you encounter the former, strip off the remaining paint and brush on wood hardener to restore its strength. If it is crumbling away, buy some two-part resin filler along with the hardener. Cut back to sound wood, paint with hardener and then fill with the resin. Even quite large sections can be restored in this way.

**3 Fill holes**
Small cracks and holes can be filled in the usual way, using an exterior grade filler. Gaps between door or window frames and surrounding masonry are best repaired with one of the gun-applied mastics, which remain flexible to cope with seasonal expansion. Also use mastic if there are gaps in the joints of a window or door.

**1 Remove flaking paint and rust**
Wherever the old paint is cracked or flaking, remove it. If it does not come away easily with a shave hook, use a hot air stripper or a blowlamp (but not on windows – a chemical stripper is best here). Remove rust from cast-iron rainwater goods or steel windows using a wire brush, preferably a power tool attachment.

**4 Re-putty windows** ▷
Check all the putty round panes of glass in windows and doors and prise out any which is loose or cracked. Paint the rebate with primer and allow to dry. Apply a 'sausage' of putty round the edge of the panes and shape to match the rest with a putty knife. Allow to dry for two weeks before painting.

> **CHECK YOUR NEEDS**
> **For painting woodwork:**
> ☐ Ladder or access tower
> ☐ Polythene sheet
> ☐ Hot air stripper, blowlamp or chemical stripper, if required
> ☐ Paint scraper and shave hooks
> ☐ Abrasive paper (wet-and-dry and ordinary glasspaper)
> ☐ Exterior filler
> ☐ Wood hardener and resin filler, if required
> ☐ Filling knife
> ☐ Stiff brush
> ☐ Paint brushes
> ☐ Paint: knotting, primer, undercoat, gloss, as necessary
> ☐ Paint kettle with hook

**5 Rub down and clean**
Rub down any filled areas, and patches of bare wood, with abrasive paper to obtain a smooth surface. Brush surface grit and dirt off the paintwork and rub it down all over with wet and dry abrasive paper, used wet. Rinse well and leave to dry.

**6 Apply primer and base coat**
Put down decorators' polythene or dust sheets to collect drips and splashes, making sure that all plants are protected. If any new wood has been used, first seal any knots in it with knotting solution to prevent the resin bleeding. Prime all areas of bare or filled wood. Allow two hours for acrylic primer to dry, 24 hours for other types. Then apply the undercoat or first coat of gloss. Use a 50mm brush for relatively large areas like fascia boards and barge boards, a 25mm brush for door and window frames and a cutting-in brush for any glazing bars.

**7 Apply finishing coat**
Rub the base coat down lightly with fine abrasive paper to remove any 'nibs' or other blemishes. Apply the top coat with even brush strokes to get a smooth finish. Do not paint too thickly, or excess paint will build up and form into sags. On windows, allow the paint to lap fractionally on to the glass to form a waterproof seal.

**8 Dealing with downpipes ▷**
When painting downpipes, protect the wall behind with a large piece of card.

**9 Painting doors**
Paint doors early in the day so that they can be left open for as long as possible afterwards. If shut before the paint hardens it will stick round the frame and spoil the finish.

## PAINTING WALLS

To ensure paint remains in good condition, repair pebbledash, rendering and rainwater goods before you start any decorating. You may also have to call in professionals to deal with any problems caused by rising damp. (Wait until the walls dry out before painting. This may take some months.)

**1 Prepare for action**
Before starting work, clear away all obstructions from the walls: trellis panels, shutters, hanging baskets etc. Clinging plants like Virginia creeper will have to be cut down to the ground (they will soon grow back); flexible climbers can be partly cut back, then laid on the ground.

**2 Clean the surface ▷**
Brush the entire wall surface to remove flaking paint, dirt and mould growth. Use a stiff hand-brush (not a wire brush as particles of metal could cause rust marks in the paint), and a paint scraper. If the surface is chalky, apply a stabilizing primer before painting. If it has been stained by rust from rainwater goods, or tar filtering out from a chimney, seal the stained areas with an aluminium primer.

**3 Treat mould growth**
Mould growth and lichen may indicate damp, which should be treated, but also occurs where no sunlight falls. To sterilize and kill off the mould, use a fungicide, or a 1:4 solution of household bleach and water. Apply with an old paint brush, leave for 48 hours, then scrub off with clean water.

**4 Prepare to paint**
Fill any cracks revealed by the cleaning processes with a proprietary external filler. Cover the ground where you are working and nearby shrubs with decorators' polythene or dust sheets. Transfer the paint into a plastic bucket or a paint trough; do not fill more than about one-third full.

### CHECK YOUR NEEDS
**For painting walls**
- ☐ Stiff brush
- ☐ Paint scraper
- ☐ Fungicide or bleach if needed
- ☐ Stabilizing primer and/or aluminium sealer, if needed
- ☐ Exterior filler
- ☐ Masonry paint or other wall finish
- ☐ Filling knife or small trowel
- ☐ Plastic bucket and S hook
- ☐ Paint tray or trough
- ☐ Large paint roller with spare sleeve
- ☐ 10-15cm exterior grade brush, preferably nylon
- ☐ Dustpan brush if required
- ☐ Polythene sheet or dust sheets
- ☐ Sponge

**5 Painting with a roller ▷**
This is the quickest, cleanest way to work but, unless working from a platform, you cannot use an ordinary paint tray and will need a special trough which hooks on to the ladder. (Alternatively, use a large brush when working above ground level, and switch to the roller once you can work from a stepladder or the ground.) Use a long-pile roller for heavily textured walls; a medium one for lightly-textured or smooth ones. Some rollers have a hollow handle so you can extend their reach by inserting a length of dowel.

Start at the top and work from right to left (unless you are left-handed). If you are not able to finish the complete wall in one session, try to stop at a natural break – an architectural feature, corner or drainpipe – so that any slight variation in colour or texture will not be noticeable.

**6 Painting with brushes** ▷
Dip the brush no more than halfway into the paint and apply it with vertical strokes, then criss-cross with horizontal ones to get even coverage. Use the bristle ends to knock paint into rough areas, and to cut into window frames or against the fascia board.

To get behind downpipes without smearing paint on them, tape on a sleeve of newspaper and push it down as you go. Wipe off any splashes on woodwork or window panes with a damp sponge as you go along. If left to dry they are very hard to get off.

**7 Painting pebbledash** ▷
With very deeply textured surfaces – pebbledash, roughcast or Tyrolean – you need to apply the paint with a stiff dustpan brush. Have the paint in a roller tray or large bucket and dab the brush in to load it with paint. Apply it to the wall using a circular scrubbing motion.

### BRIGHT IDEA

**Keep it clean** If your house is on a busy road, dirt and fumes from the traffic can quickly make the paintwork shabby. While you still have the ladder or access tower in use, spray the gloss-painted woodwork with silicone polish and buff up to repel dirt.

## REDECORATING YOUR HOUSE: WHAT'S INVOLVED

**A** Chimneys and roof: check for repairs
**B** Rainwater goods: clean out gutters and repair where necessary. Derust and paint cast-iron ones; do not paint plastic
**C** Soffit (board under overhang): clean and apply two coats of emulsion
**D** Barge boards, fascia boards: prepare, prime, apply base coat and finishing coat
**E** Painted brickwork, stonework or rendering: brush down, fill cracks, stabilize if chalky, sterilize mould, seal stains, apply two coats of wall finish
**F** Brickwork: brush down, repoint as necessary. Do not paint
**G** Cladding: if stained or varnished, rub down and apply a similar finish. If painted, treat as for doors and windows. Wash PVC cladding
**H** Porches and subsidiary roofs: protect from spilled paint with dust sheets
**J** Timber windows, doors: prepare, prime and paint; or recoat natural timber finish
**K** Metal windows, garage doors: derust, prime and paint. Do not paint aluminium door or window frames

### LADDER SAFETY

**REMEMBER:** Falls are one of the major causes of DIY accidents.
**DO** Use a ladder at least 60cm taller than the highest point to be painted.
**DO** Secure the ladder – with stakes, a sandbag or rope.
**DO** Wear lace-up boots or shoes with a proper heel. Avoid getting them slippery with mud by placing a door mat at the foot of the ladder.
**DO** Overlap ladder sections by at least one quarter of their length.
**DO** Use a ladder stay to hold the ladder away from the wall if you have to paint overhanging eaves or the guttering, otherwise you will have to lean back dangerously.
**DON'T** Place the ladder less than 30cm away from the wall for every 120cm of its height.
**DON'T** Climb higher than four rungs from the top; you must always be able to hold on to the ladder.
**DON'T** Lean the ladder against gutters, drainpipes, or glass.
**DON'T** Lean out sideways when painting – move the ladder.
**DON'T** Work on a windy day.

# EXTERIOR DOOR FURNITURE

Whether fitting a new front door or smartening up an existing one, the right door fittings complete the picture.

When choosing furniture for exterior doors, the two most important points to bear in mind are whether it is right for the style of the door, and whether it is rugged enough to stand up to extremes of weather, year after year.

Front doors are usually equipped with more imposing fittings than those used at the back, but – like front door fittings – they too need to be weatherproof and should be in the right style.

**Materials** Any metal that doesn't rust can be used for exterior door furniture. The traditional choices are brass or black iron. Bronze, which is rather more expensive, is not widely used, and brass (lacquered to prevent tarnishing) is still popular today. But modern metals, such as anodized aluminium or chrome-plated metal, are equally durable.

For the best effect, all front door furniture should match, and this is easiest to achieve with metal fittings. However, modern plastic furniture is just as hard-wearing, and the heavy-duty nylon ranges are ideal for outdoors.

**Style** First make sure the front door looks right. Apart from its main functions: security, privacy and insulation, it should also suit the character of the house. The next step is to choose the right door furniture. Generally, plain styles suit modern doors, and the more ornate ones look best on period designs.

Brass door furniture is made in so many different styles that it can suit almost any type of house and door. Decorative black iron is best suited to old oak doors or country properties, but plainer designs can look good on panelled doors fitted to town houses.

Anodized aluminium or chromed fittings can look modern or very traditional, depending on the style of the door itself. Coloured nylon fittings give a super-modern look.

## WHAT TO BUY

It is possible to furnish a front door with one item – a vertical postal knocker with provision for a lock – but you can have as many as half a dozen. Whatever style and finish you choose, make sure they come from the same manufacturer and are an exact match.

Popular brass and aluminium styles can be bought in hardware packs containing handles, all fittings, and a lock. But some of the more burglar-proof locks are available only from a locksmith. Study the door before buying fittings to make sure they will fit and are in the right style. The letter opening in an old door may be much too small; take the opportunity to enlarge it.

**Centre door knobs** (centre pulls) These are heavyweight versions of the mortice knob used on interior doors, sold singly instead of in pairs. They are fitted by means of a long screw which goes through the centre stile of the door.

**Cylinder pulls and roses** These are an alternative to a knob, when the door has a cylindrical lock (operated with a Yale-type key and fitted into a large hole bored through the door). A cylinder cover can be fitted to this.

**Lever lock handles** These can be obtained in a wide variety of styles and finishes to suit any type of house or door. They are identical to the interior type. Nowadays however, these are not often found on front doors but may be used on back doors with a bolt.

**Door knockers** Now that most houses have electric bells, knockers are not really necessary but they do provide a means of shutting the door behind you if there is no knob or cylinder pull. And they give such character to a front door, and come in such wonderful designs, that they are hard to resist. However ornate, they simply use a hinged ring or bar of metal to knock on a metal striking plate.

**Letter plates** These consist of a rectangular metal plate secured to the front of the door with an opening cut in it and a hinged flap covering the opening. Spring flap letter plates open inwards; gravity flap ones open outwards. They are usually fitted horizontally, but vertical designs are available for use on glazed doors where this is not possible. A draught excluder (or flap) can be fitted inside.

**Postal knocker** Essentially the same as letter plates, these incorporate a metal bar or ring which is both door knocker and pull handle in one. Vertical designs can also have a lock hole.

**Bell pushes** A front door does not have to have the commonly-fitted plastic door bell push. They can be bought to match the rest of the door furniture.

**Number plates** Numbers from 0-9 can be obtained to match any type of door furniture. Some ranges also include letters for building up numbers like 1A. The best brass numbers are fitted by studs on the back so that screws do not disfigure the surface. Plastic numbers and letters are widely available and some simply stick on. Although much cheaper they tend not to look as good, or last as long, as metal ones, unless they are of heavy-duty nylon.

**Name plates** are usually fitted beside rather than on the door, and can be made of brass, pottery, wood, slate, or enamelled metal. They are used to accommodate a house name (sometimes a number as well) and make it both noticeable and decorative.

**Escutcheons** Where a door is closed with a deadlock, this can be protected with an escutcheon.

## DOOR FURNITURE STYLES

### BLACK IRON

**Style** This highly distinctive type of door furniture is based on designs used from the 16th century onwards, and is also known as antique, Tudor, or Elizabethan ironwork. All items have a hammered black finish, but some are very Gothic in style, adorned with fleur-de-lys motifs or heart shapes, while others are quite plain.

**Watchpoint** Black iron furniture has a very strong character and should be used sparingly, otherwise it can overwhelm the door. However, it is ideal for Tudor, Victorian, or Gothic-style properties.

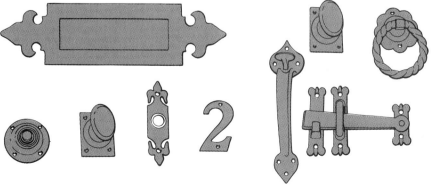

### GEORGIAN BRASS
**Style** Different manufacturers have different interpretations of this, but the common feature is a ropework edging; lever handles are curved and finished with a scroll. Although a letter plate would not have been fitted in the 18th century, 'period' styles are available to accommodate the demands of the 20th century.
**Watchpoint** As with all brass furniture for outdoor use, it is best to pick solid brass. Although expensive it lasts indefinitely, which brass plate cannot be expected to do.

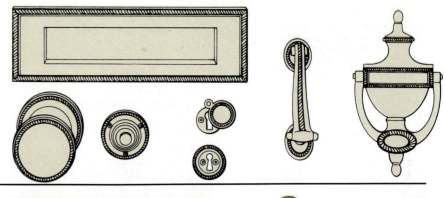

### REGENCY STYLE
**Style** Although this dates from within the Georgian period (from about 1810) and is basically similar to the Georgian style, it is more decorative in style. The edging motif is pearl beading rather than ropework.
**Watchpoint** Like Georgian brass, Regency fittings look out of place on heavy-looking doors of the Tudor or Jacobean type and is especially unsuitable for Victorian or Gothic-style houses. But it can look good on a modern, fully or partly-glazed mahogany door.

### VICTORIAN METAL
**Style** Although the Gothic style saw a revival during the Victorian period, door furniture used in these times was generally much plainer in style and was usually without borders. Victorian style fittings give an impression of solidity, and an imposing knocker is an important feature. Although brass is the most popular metal used, the same designs can be bought chrome-plated or with a bronze 'antique' finish.
**Watchpoint** For true Victorian character fit a door knob and/or knocker.

### ROCOCO
**Style** Essentially a very ornate French style which originated in the mid 18th century. Although door furniture made in this style for use outdoors has to be considerably more robust than anything used inside, it echoes the Fancy Filigree or Ormolu type of door furniture which is used indoors.
**Watchpoint** Very decorative and rather fancy in style so not really suited to modern houses or on doors where the style is simple. It is also extremely expensive.

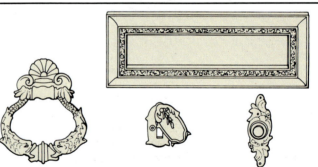

### MODERN METAL
**Style** If you want brass door furniture, but your house and door are modern, fittings with clean modern lines are available or the plain Victorian designs will serve perfectly well. But the most modern-looking fittings of all are those made in anodized aluminium. Chrome-plated furniture is another option – it is not widely stocked but can be obtained to order.
**Watchpoint** If you have a modern aluminium-framed glazed door, matching anodized aluminium furniture is essential.

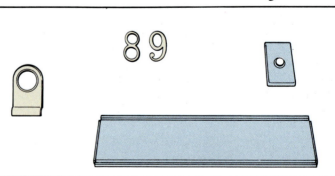 

### PLASTIC
**Style** As the material is modern, so too is the style of the door furniture that is made from it. There are two distinct types: heavy-duty nylon furniture (architect-designed and quite expensive); and the cheap plastic knobs which are found in hardware shops. The former comes in bright primary colours and will give unique character to a modern house fitted with a modern door. The cheaper type of plastic usually comes in white, black, or brown only, but will serve for a back door or shed.

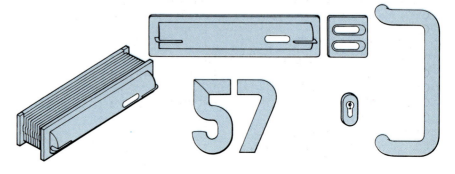

# INDEX

## A
Access hatch
  to plumbing, 36
  to underfloor surfaces, 75
Adhesives
  for floor tiles, 69
  for wood, 39, 40, 41
Ageing (distressing)
  metals, 66
  wood, 49
Alcoves
  fitting shelving, 14
  panelling, 34
Aluminium, door furniture, 93-4
Architraves, 29-30, 31, 34, 38
Ash, 55, 75

## B
Bath panels, 36, 74
Battens, 9, 14, 33-6
Beading, 38
  for doors, 17, 19, 25, 27, 28
  for floors, around edges, 70, 73
  for panelling, 36
Beech, 55, 75
Bell pushes, 93
Bits, for drills, 8, 10
Blacklead, 59, 61, 62
Bleach, for wood, 47, 49, 85, 86
Blockboard, shelves, 11-12
Blowlamps/torches, 47, 60, 90
Brackets, for shelves, 11-12, 13, 15-16
Bradawls, 7, 10
Brass, 63-6
  door furniture, 93-4
Bronze, 63-6
  door furniture, 93-4

## C
Cables, electrical, locating, 35
Cast-iron, decorating, 89, 90
Catches, cupboard doors, 25, 26
Cedar, 33
Ceilings, attaching fixtures to, 9
Cellulose thinner, 44
Chair rails see Dado rails
Chairs, wooden, repair, 39-42
Cherrywood, 55
Chimney, maintenance, 87
China, door fittings, 10
Chipboard
  shelves, 11
  woodstrip flooring, 76, 80, 82
Chrome, door furniture, 93-4
Cladding
  artificial stone, 87-8
  wooden, tongued-and-grooved, 33-6
Concrete floors, 68, 71, 76
Copper, renovation, 63-4
Cork tiles, 67-70
Cornice moulding, 37
Corroless, rust treatment, 61, 62
Cupboard doors see Doors, cupboard

## D
Dado, panelled, 33, 34
Dado rails (chair rails), 29-30, 32, 38
Damp course, 87-8
Damp, rising, 91
Door stop, repositioning, 19, 38
Door
  clearance, 68, 76, 80
  cupboard, renovation, 25-8
  external, painting, 91, 92
  external, replacement, 88
  furniture, 23, 63, 65, 93-4
  renovation/repair, 17-20, 21-4
Dowel moulding, 38
Downpipes
  maintenance, 87-8
  painting, 89-92
Drawer linings, 46
Drills, 7-10
Dyes, wood, 48, 49, 50, 86

## E
Ear defenders, 83, 84
Edge nosing, 38
Edging strips, iron-on, for wood, 13
Eggshell paint, 51, 52, 54
Elm, 55, 75
Enamels
  for brass, 63
  for coating iron or steel, 61
Escutcheons, 93

## F
Face mask, for dusty jobs, 83, 84
Facings, flush, on doors, removal, 18
Fibreglass, for metal repairs, 61
Filler
  external, for cracks and holes, 90-1
  grain filler, 47-9, 57
  for holes in floorboards, 86
  for ironwork, 61
  for wood sheet flooring, 82
  for woodwork, 36
Fireplaces, 34, 59, 63, 66
Flashing, maintenance, 87-8
Floorcoverings
  sheet, 71-4
  surface preparation, 68, 71, 76
  tiles, 67-70
  wood, 75-82, 83-6
French polish, 43, 44, 45, 55-8
Furniture
  finishing, 55-8
  renovation, 43-6, 51-4
  see also Chairs

## G
Glass shelves, 12, 15
Glass fibre, for metal repairs, 61
Glazes, 51, 52, 54
Glazing bead, 38
Grain filler, 47-9, 57
Graphite powder, 24
Grate polish see Blacklead
Gutters, maintenance, 87-8, 89

## H
Half-round moulding, 38

Handles
  brass or wood, 46
  fitting, to doors, 23
  lever lock, 93
  new, for cupboard doors, 25, 28
Hardboard
  as base for floor tiles, 68
  and wood effect flooring, 76, 80, 82
Hardwood, 55, 83, 86
Hardwood strip flooring, 75-8
Hinges, 21, 22, 24
  on cupboard doors, 25, 26, 27

## I
Insulation
  behind panelling, 33, 35, 36
  underfloor, 83
Iroko, 75, 79
Iron, ironwork
  decorating, 90
  door furniture, 93
  renovation, 59-62

## J
Joints
  mitred, 19
  mortice and tenon, 17
  wooden, repair, 39, 40, 41
Joists, and ceiling fixtures, 9

## K
Knotting solution, 33, 36, 90, 91

## L
Lacquer, for metals, 63, 65
Laminates
  for cupboard doors, 27, 28
  for shelves, 46
Light fittings, repositioning, 33-6
Liming, wood, 58
Linoleum, laying, 71-4
Linseed oil, 43, 44, 58
Lipping, timber, 13, 38
Locks, lubrication, 24

## M
Mahogany, 55, 83
  doors, 17
  tongued-and-grooved panelling, 33
  woodstrip flooring, 75, 79, 80
Maple, 55, 75
Masonry, maintenance, 89, 90
Mastic, 90
Meranti, 33
Merbau, 75, 79
Methylated spirit, 44, 58
Mitre boxes, 19, 29, 32
Mitred corners/joints, 30-2
Mortar, repair, 88
Mosaic floor tiles, 79-82
Mould, on exterior walls, 87, 91
Mouldings, wood, 37-8
  replacement, 29-32
Muntins (vertical door members), 17

## N
Nylon, door furniture, 93-4

## O

Oak, 55, 83
    doors, 17
    woodstrip flooring, 75, 79, 80
Oil
    for coating metals, 59, 61, 62
    for furniture, 43, 55
    for squeaking doors, 24
    for wood, 48, 50
Ovolo door stop, 38

## P

Paintbrushes
    for external paints, 90-2
    for varnishing, 48
Paints
    for brass, copper and bronze, 63, 65
    for iron and steel, 59, 61, 62
    for exterior work, 90
    stripping, 47
    for wooden panelling, 33, 36
Panelling, wooden, 33-6, 37
Panels, on doors, 17-20
Parquet flooring
    see Floorcoverings, wood
Pebbledash, 91-2
Picture rails, 29-30, 32, 37
Pine doors, 17
Pipes, 63, 65, 73, 78, 81
Plastic, door furniture, 93-4
Plywood
    shelves, 11-12
    wood effect flooring, 80, 82
Polish, for brass and copper, 65
Polyurethane varnish see Varnish
Power points, repositioning, 33-6
Primer, 90-1
    metal, 59, 61
Profile gauge, 68, 70, 73
Putty, for glazing, 90
PVC self-adhesive sheeting, 46

## Q

Quadrant beading, 36, 38, 76, 78, 81

## R

Radiator enamel, 61
Rails (horizontal door members), 17
Rendering, maintenance, 87, 89, 90, 91
Rising butt hinges, 21, 22
Roof maintenance, 87
Rosewood, 55
Rot, 83, 87, 88, 90
Rust, 59, 60, 61

## S

Safety goggles, 83, 84
Sanders, 36, 56-7, 83-6
Sapele, wood effect flooring, 80
Saws, 29, 84
Scotch glue see Adhesives, for wood
Scotia beading/moulding, 36, 38
Screed, screeding mortar, 68
Screwdrivers, 21
Screws, 7-10, 12
Sealant, for floors, 67
Secret nailing, 75
Sheet flooring, laying, 79-82
Shellac, 57
Shelves, 11-14, 15-16
    in kitchen, 7
    for ornaments, 34
Shiplap moulding, 37
Skirting, 29-31, 34, 37, 76, 80-1
Slates, on roof, checking, 87, 88
Softwood, 55
    tongued-and-grooved panelling, 33
    see also Flooring
Spirit level, 12, 13, 14, 35, 36
Square-edge moulding, 38
Stainers, for wood, 33, 36, 47, 51, 55-7, 86
Steel
    decorating, 90
    renovation, 59-62
Steel wool, 59, 60
Stencilling, on hardboard floors, 82
Stiles (vertical door members), 17
Strippers
    chemical, for iron and steel, 60
    liquid, for brass and copper, 64-5
    paint, 47-50, 56, 90

## T

Taps, brass, 63
Teak, flooring, 79, 80, 83
Teak oil, 43
Tiles, roof, checking, 87-8
Tiling floors, 67-70, 75-82
Timber lipping, 13, 38
Tints see Stainers
Tongued-and-grooved boards, 33-6, 37
Tools and equipment
    for fixing screws to walls, 7-8
    for laying floorcovering, 72
    for outside decorating, 89-90, 91
    for renovating iron and steel, 59
    for renovating wood floors, 83
    for repairing doors, 21
    for replacing wood mouldings, 29
    for refinishing wood, 47-8
    for tiling, 68
Try square, 8
Turpentine, 44

## V

Varnish, 43, 44, 45
    for coating iron and steel, 59
    for wooden floors, 78, 79-80, 86
    polyurethane, 44-5, 51-4
        for sealing cork tiles, 67, 68, 70
        for wood, 33, 36, 48, 50, 55
    stripping, 47
Veneer, 48
    for finishing shelves, 13
    trims, 28
    for wood flooring, 75, 79
Ventilation, underfloor, 83
Verdigris, 63, 65
Vinyl floorcoverings, 67-70, 71-4

## W

Wallplugs, 7-8, 9, 12
Walls
    panelled, 33-6
    exterior, maintenance, 87-92
    fixing screws into, 7-10
    mounting shelves, 11-14
    type of, identification test, 7
Walnut, 55
Waterproofing, external, 89
Wax, filler for wood, 45
Wax polish, 43-5, 47-8, 50, 55
Weatherbar, 37
White spirit, 44
Window frames, 59, 88-9, 92
Wire brushes, 59, 60, 61
Wire wool, 59, 60
Wood
    liming, 58
    mouldings, 37-8
    shelves, 11, 15
    stripping and refinishing, 47-50
    swollen, causing sticking, 24
    see also Furniture
Wooden flooring, 75-8, 79-80
Woodstopping, 47
Woodwork
    decorating trims, 32
    exterior, decorating, 89-92
    replacement, 29-32
Woodworm, 30, 43-4, 83
Workbench, portable, 39

---

PHOTOGRAPHIC CREDITS
Front cover Next Interior, Texas Homecare, Arthur Sanderson and Sons, Be Modern Ltd, 1 EWA, 2-3 Dulux Woodcare, 4-5 Ideal Standard, 6 Homecharm, 7 Crown Paints, 10 Designers Guild, 11 Spectrum Shelving, 14 EWA/Tom Leighton, 20 The Picture Library, 21 Arthur Sanderson and Sons, 25 EWA/Michael Dunne, 29 PWA International, 32 Jerry Tubby/Eaglemoss, 33 Arthur Sanderson and Sons, 36 Dulux paints, 39 EWA/Michael Nicholson, 43 John Suett/Eaglemoss, 46 Coloroll, 47 Syndication International, 50 Coloroll, 51 Royal Pavilion, Brighton, 54 EWA/Michael Dunne, 55 Coloroll, 58 EWA/Michael Dunne, 59 The Cast Iron Fireplace Company, 62 Correless, 63 Dorma, 66 Stovax, 67 Concork, 70 Amtico, 71 Forbo-Nairn, 75 Simon Butcher/Eaglemoss, 78 Ron Sutherland, 79 EWA/Tom Leighton, 82 Conran Octopus/Peter Mackertich (Designer Tony Mackertich), 83 Martin Goodard, 86 Dulux Woodcare, 89 Crown Plus Two

ILLUSTRATIONS
David Ashby, Craig Austen, Mike Fisher (Garden Studios), Hayward and Martin, Kevin Jones Associates, Kuo Kang Chen, Stan North, Ross Wardle (Portland Artists)